Natural Environment Research Council

Land use mapping
by local authorities
in Britain

A report commissioned by
the Department of the Environment
and prepared by the
EXPERIMENTAL CARTOGRAPHY UNIT

The Architectural Press
1978

c   Natural Environment Research Council 1978

First published by the Architectural Press Ltd: London 1978
ISBN 0   85139 333 0

Printed in England
Text and maps by Gavin Martin Limited.

PREFACE

This report, completed in 1976 by the Experimental Cartography Unit (ECU) of the Natural Environment Research Council, records the findings and recommendations of the ECU resulting from an investigation funded by the Department of the Environment into land use mapping in local authorities in Great Britain.

The report is made available for information only. The opinions and recommendations expressed in the report are not necessarily those of the Department and should not be considered as advice from the Department for any course of action to be taken. In particular, it is recognised that the report makes no detailed analysis of the financial implications of its recommendations and does not take account of current restraints on local authority expenditure.

It should be noted that the Valuation Office proposals described in the report for the future computerisation of their records, including the use of VOPREN and the coded description system, are provisional. The Government has issued a Green Paper (May 1977) in response to the Layfield Committee's report and has announced that a revaluation based on rental value will be conducted in 1982. In the meantime, the Department of the Environment is holding discussions with the IRVO on the computerisation plans including the grid referencing of hereditaments.

A.E. Seddon
Director, Scientific & Technical Services
Natural Environment Research Council.

July 1978

ACKNOWLEDGEMENTS

Cartography tends to result from the work of a group rather than an individual, and this has also been the case with this research project. Many people were involved in the various stages of this study and they are too numerous to cite individually. However, some particular acknowledgements are necessary.

First among these is Dr. Fraser Taylor of the Department of Geography at Carleton University, Ottawa, who has special interests in digital cartography and who worked as a leading member of the ECU team.

Secondly, we note the advice and help given to us at a critical stage of our work by Sir Frank Layfield.

Thirdly, we record the assistance which we received from the Inland Revenue Valuation Office, and in particular from Mr. N. Behr and Mr. L. Tapper.

Fourthly, we record the helpfulness, patience and good humour of those Local Authority Planning Departments who acted as our "samples": we especially acknowledge Mr. Terry Gould of Hampshire County Council and Mr. David Challen of Cheshire County Council.

Finally, we take particular note of the meticulous digitising, processing, plotting, etc. of the sample maps (Appendix I) largely carried out by our colleague Mr. A. W. Clifton. These maps are, of course, the result of equipments, software and techniques developed by the ECU over a decade. In this case they have provided overprints to Ordnance Survey base maps, which have served this function admirably in their standard, non-digital, form.

Experimental Cartography Unit   David Bickmore
Natural Environment Research Council   Ann Molineux

July 1978

CONTENTS

LAND USE MAPPING BY LOCAL AUTHORITIES IN BRITAIN

1. ## Scope of Project

1.1   In April 1975 agreement was reached between the Department of the Environment (DOE) and the Natural Environment Research Council (NERC) on a study of the ways in which land use information is used by local planning authorities. The study has been carried out by NERC's Experimental Cartography Unit (ECU). The project began early in 1975, and the final report was submitted to DOE by late 1976.

1.2   The rationale for the study has been concisely set out by DOE in the following terms:

> "Many local authorities are known to experience difficulty in acquiring and storing detailed information about land use, whether in map or statistical form: recording change in land use may often be found particularly difficult. Where information is available in map form there may also be difficulty in retrieving and using it when required, especially at short notice. At this time of progress in computer data management systems and with local government settling down into its restructured form, it would seem wise to ascertain the current, and if possible the potential, need to make land use data readily accessible within the authority. Additionally, it would be useful to know whether such data should be handled by conventional means or through automated procedures, and whether the most useful information is cartographic or tabular in nature. There is therefore a case for studying the need for and the operational problems of using land use information by the planning departments of individual local authorities."

1.3   It was decided that ECU, using a set of 15 local planning authorities,

> ".... should investigate how local authorities currently gather, store and utilise land use information and how far they see a need for an automated system, which would allow freer cross-referencing with other digital records available to a local planning authority."
> (DOE 1975)

1.4   The following authorities were selected by DOE on the basis that they were

       ".... a fair cross section of the different types of authorities undertaking planning functions. " (DOE 1975).

County Councils:	Cheshire
	Gwent
	Hampshire
	Merseyside
	Mid Glamorgan
	Norfolk
Districts:	East Lothian
	Edinburgh
London Boroughs:	Kensington & Chelsea
	Lambeth
Metropolitan Districts:	Birmingham
	Coventry
	Leeds
	Manchester
	Newcastle-upon-Tyne

1.5   A prime function of the survey was to visit these authorities and to record detailed notes about land use and associated topics as a result of discussion with the officers concerned. A copy of each of these site reports was sent for comment and checking by the authority, and a close and easy liaison between ECU and the authorities was maintained. A valuable 'workshop' session to discuss an interim report was held in the ECU in February 1976; it was attended by representatives of each of the authorities involved. The interest, helpfulness and courtesy of the authorities invariably exceeded all expectation.

1.6   The ECU survey was to be aimed

       ".... essentially at current practice and needs of local authorities in mapping land use data: 'land use' for the purpose of this project.. (was) taken to mean primarily those uses controlled by the Town and Country Planning Acts". (DOE 1975).

Section 11 (i) of the Town and Country Planning Act defines development as

       ".... the carrying out of building, engineering, mining or other operations in, on, over and under land, or the making of any material change in the use of any building or other land. "

Thus "operations" and "uses" of land are stressed. Note that agriculture and forestry are excluded.

1. 7 It is important in this context to draw attention to the detailed nature of "development" because this generally calls for very large scale mapping, e.g. to discriminate between different uses in adjacent buildings or between different activities at various floor levels in a large building. For this degree of detail, base map scales such as 1:1250 or 1:2500 (as provided by the Ordnance Survey) are necessary. This kind of high resolution land use mapping, with which this report has been concerned, is thus in some contrast to the much smaller scales used in displaying agricultural or environmental factors, as for example in the Second Land Utilisation Survey of Great Britain or in NERC's "Ecobase" computer mapping project.

1. 8 As instructed by DOE, the ECU survey concentrated on the planning departments of 15 selected local authorities. As the survey progressed it became evident that land use information was sometimes collected and stored by other departments within authorities, and some information from these sources was obtained, e.g. from Central Research and Intelligence Units and from joint studies. However, a comprehensive search of all sources of information bearing on the use of land within all departments of authorities was beyond both ECU's terms of reference and the resources and time available. It is clear too that information about the use of land is also significant to many public and private agencies outside local authorities; for example, public utilities are both contributors and users of such information. However, a study of these sources was also beyond the terms of reference of this project and, except in the particular case of the Valuation Lists of the Inland Revenue (and the derived Ratings Lists in local authorities), this was not developed.

2. Planning requirements for land use

2. 1 Development control. Proposals for any change in land use are a major concern in all authorities, and the survey revealed a definite need for detailed - i.e. property-by-property information about land use for development control purposes. It is important to emphasise that this concern with change of use obviously relates only to a small proportion of the land in an authority and is distinct from the wide geographical context assumed by land use mapping. Nevertheless, planning officials are faced with many hundreds of thousands of applications for change of use, most of them of the detailed "physical planning" type: indeed, development control has been described as the "trenches" of British planning. Many officials realise the need for ensuring that the patterns emerging as a result of a series of individual decisions should be monitored in addition to the calculation of change in total floor space or acreage, which is presently a requirement. In theory, as development control decisions are taken within a framework established by zoning policy, the emerging patterns should be predictable to a large degree.

In practice, many of the approved development plans were prepared several years ago and, although amendments have been made, the current relevance of these documents seems somewhat questionable. In some areas, many of the development control decisions taken are incompatible with existing zoning regulations. This situation would seem less likely to develop if up to date land use maps - as opposed to statistics - were widely available.

2.2   Structure Plans.   The new Structure Plan established new statutory guidelines, but in few areas have these yet (1976) been approved. In the interim the actual pattern on the ground is changing. Large applications for change of land use tend to be considered in relation to their structure plan implications; small applications do not. How many small applications, approved on a one-by-one basis, are required before a pattern of wider planning significance emerges? It would seem logical for such patterns to be considered at both structure and local planning levels in the monitoring process. Here is another need for the land use map, as opposed to statistical measures such as floor space; there is no other easy way in which such patterns can be monitored.

2.3   Structure planning itself seems to be approached in a variety of ways, and the role of the land use map is affected by the interpretation used. A Structure Plan is primarily a policy document and attempts to avoid issues of detailed locational significance. Consequently, some authorities, e.g. Gwent, are giving little consideration to the inclusion of locationally specific data in policy formation. With this approach to plan preparation, the role of the map is not great. Other authorities, e.g. Mid Glamorgan, use the map as an analytical tool in the preparation of the Structure Plan, with the ward or parish as the smallest spatial unit. They are thus aware of the broader spatial patterns and the implications that the policy they suggest will have on these. A few authorities, e.g. Merseyside, usually where relatively little land is available for development purposes, are concerned with the detailed spatial implications of their policies. Here the map plays a large part in the planning process.

2.4   Community Land Act.   This Act of 1975 is clearly liable to affect land use, and to affect it in quantitative - financial - terms. During the survey stage of the project in 1975 little mention was made of this new Act, since its implications had not then been studied. However, by early 1976 several authorities expressed the view that their priorities in terms of land use change might well be altered as a result of the implications of the Act.

2.5   Detailed data about land values seems basic to this point, and the report of the Committee of Enquiry into Local Government Finance (Layfield Report Cmd 6453 - May 1976) also has indirect relevance to the problems of land use. The report recommends some changes in the methods of assessing rateable value (e.g. that assessments of domestic property should be based on capital value and not on rental); also on the inclusion within the rating system of certain types of property previously excluded (Crown lands and agricultural land) and in the frequency of revaluations. At present, planning departments in local authorities do not make extensive use of Rating Lists as a source of land use information; nevertheless, these lists do supply quantifiable information (value) on the scale of detail required and over the entire area. We return to an assessment of the potential of the Valuation List/Rating File as a source of land use information in a later section of this report and in Appendix II.

2.6   Land use sometimes suffers from being a broad and ill-defined subject, and there are many instances, not surprisingly, where planners are handling data of locational significance which are not specifically labelled as of land use data: this is also true for the social service departments and for the highway and engineering departments. Land use in this wider sense seems regarded as a part of the corpus of knowledge necessary to the general management of a modern authority.

2.7   DOE requirements for land use information. A circular of April 1974 (Circ 71/74) directs all local authorities to furnish annual statistics of land use change. These statistics have to be arranged in the following 15 categories (which are groupings used in the National Land Use Classification):

1.	Agriculture & Fisheries	9.	Residences
2.	Community & Health Services	10.	Retail Distribution & Servicing
3.	Defence		
4.	Education	11.	Storage
5.	Recreation & Leisure	12.	Transport
6.	Manufacturing	13.	Utility Services
7.	Mineral Extraction	14.	Wholesale Distribution
8.	Offices	15.	Unused Land, Water & Buildings.

These annual returns of change are required down to the level of District Councils and London Boroughs. This relatively limited geographical breakdown is evidently sufficient for central government, but seems to have limited value in itself for local authority planning. The authorities are able to compile figures of change as a result of collating their Development Control information (see 2.1).

We have pointed out that Development Control information may not reflect very accurately the true land use picture in an area and will not, on its own, give the context in which changes are taking place in relation to present day land use nor to future patterns envisaged by Structure Plans. As a result of this one may question whether the statistics that are furnished annually to DOE "remedy.... the serious deficiency of information on land use" that circular 71/74 seeks to address. Over and above the annual statistics of land use change, local authorities supply regular returns of Housing Completions which have obvious relevance to land use change. It is also assumed that they will be able to answer intermittent requests about land available for industrial, commercial and residential use and for the total area of derelict land. They derive such information from comparing planning permissions with development plans; however, our enquiries indicated that these plans were often seriously out of date (see 2.1) and could sometimes not be regarded as giving binding commitments to an uncertain future.

3. The traditional land use map

3.1 The survey revealed that the traditional land use map, recording existing land use typically by different colours, was rarely being used in the planning process - or indeed elsewhere. Only five local authorities in our survey (Lambeth, Kensington & Chelsea, Birmingham, Newcastle and Manchester) had comprehensive land use information which had been collected later than 1970. In some cases the last comprehensive survey was done in the 1960s, and in one case in the 1950s. Hand-coloured base maps at scales varying from 1:1250 to 1:10,560 existed for some of the earlier surveys, but few of the authorities considered the production of such manuscript maps to be a high priority, and none was contemplating printing and publishing them in colour.

3.2 We deduced a number of reasons why such traditional land use maps seemed to be of limited value, and these are:

(a) The costs of the full scale ad hoc survey required to provide the data for such maps are high.

(b) The data, even when collected, are constantly outdated by changing situations which render the draft maps historical documents. The process of updating and revising them, although not as expensive as the initial survey, is still significant.

(c) Even where surveys have been carried out and draft maps are available, the preparation and reproduction of coloured maps of this type is slow and increasingly expensive.

(d) Such maps, in their traditional manually prepared form, lack scale flexibility, and significant costs are involved in obtaining a synoptic picture of, e.g. a county or district from the multiplicity of large scale sheets involved.

(e) The amount of analysis possible from such maps is limited. The data on them are not quantifiable, at a time when planning appears increasingly interested in quantities.

3.3   Added to these reasons - perhaps because of them - we observed with surprise how much the level of <u>graphic awareness</u> varied between authorities, between departments and between individuals. In only one authority, East Lothian, was the map in any way central to the process by which information on land use was managed. Other exceptions were the LONEX PROJECT in Cheshire and the work of the ecological group in Merseyside, but these were offset by examples where knowledge and use of maps were very low indeed.

3.4   This variability seemed also reflected in the use of special maps for committee work and in more general matters of "public participation". At one end of the scale there are places like Kensington & Chelsea where, more often than not, if any officer wants to use a map for display or for report purposes he has to prepare it himself; at the other end of the scale there is the large, well equipped drawing office of Mid Glamorgan with an annual operating budget in the region of £100,000. Authorities like Cheshire use the map in committee as a matter of course; others like Lambeth hardly at all. The evidence collected during the survey suggests that the use of maps as display tools is limited at present by a lack of resources to produce maps quickly, and in some instances by a lack of knowledge. There seems little evidence, apart from studies by P. Stringer (University of Surrey) about map reading ability on the part of planning committees or the general public.* If the use of maps is to grow in planning, this problem may require more attention. It is one which, on the one hand, seems unlikely to be solved by dicta on standardisation of colours or symbols, and on the other hand, may be helped by the ability to produce specialised but simple overlay maps.

3.5   It may well be natural to a group concerned with cartography to deplore any shortfall in the cartographic approach to land use management problems. However, it would be ironic if the advent of the computer and of statistically oriented planners lay behind any tendency to abandon the land use map as a management tool. It was noted, however, that Central Intelligence and Research Units have been established in some authorities like Mid Glamorgan and Newcastle, and many of these units tend to be wholly oriented to statistics. In none of the large computer-based information systems which are being built up has the map been effectively integrated, and in most it has not been integrated at all. Those who have had so much difficulty themselves in having computer-based informations accepted may in their turn require convincing that the quantitative, thematic map can be used in overall information management as an integral part of the data system and not merely as an afterthought for cosmetic purposes.

---

* Stringer states (personal communication) that the Structure Plan Key Diagram poses particular problems of comprehension. It is an abstract document difficult to appreciate when the reader is unused to dealing with abstract maps.

4.   Need for land use information

4.1   DOE have particularly asked for evidence of the need for land use information by local authorities. In fact, local authorities did not come out with a clear statement about their land use needs: instead, they described what they were doing. We cannot but conclude from their statements that the need for land use information, rightly or wrongly, is not at the top of their priority list. This is not the same as saying there is a lack of need, for need itself is extremely difficult to define in this context. There was, of course, no question but that the planning system was working in all the fifteen sample local authorities in the study, and this despite relatively meagre amounts of land use data in some of them. But might it have worked better? It was no part of our survey to question the effectiveness of the planning system itself; indeed, such a question would have had to assume agreed criteria by which the success of planning could be measured. It seems to follow that if one can neither measure success rates in planning nor associate them with the presence or absence of land use information, statements about "need" for land use cannot be more than assertions.

4.2   Our assertions, therefore, on the evidence of this survey are, first that there is a natural relationship between the use of information and the feasibility and cost of gathering it regularly, reliably and in adequate detail. If this gathering can happen, the information will be used; if used intelligently, it has excellent prospects of becoming one of the essential management tools.

4.3   Our second assertion is that land use information must be location-specific in a detailed sense, probably in terms of individual hereditaments. This locational element in land use information points strongly to cartography as the prime - but not the only - medium in which land use problems should be studied. But a slow, expensive or inflexible cartography may of itself vitiate this process.

4.4   Our third assertion is that complexity of the land use picture in the urban context is too great, the number of detailed facts too large, the time requirements too short, to be manipulated solely in the human mind. Hence computing methods seem inevitable, but only if in the first place the data can be gathered.

5.   Ordnance Survey Maps

5.1   Any apparent demise of land use and thematic mapping by planners is in contrast to the use of topographical maps and plans. Ordnance Survey maps are clearly of central importance in all local authorities; their products are extensively used, and the need for updated base maps is as great as ever.

5.2   In urban areas the main scales in use are 1:1250 and 1:2500, and these maps are most frequently used for control and locational purposes.   Base maps at these scales are a statutory requirement in applications for planning permission.   Smaller scale Ordnance Survey maps at 1:25,000 and 1:50,000 are used for synoptic planning purposes and broader distributions in both urban and rural areas. The Ordnance Survey printed map is the base which is naturally assumed where distributions of special interest to local authorities have to be illustrated, e.g. in committees.

5.3   Most authorities expressed appreciation of the efforts of the OS to provide them with up to date maps; several expressed appreciation of the efforts of the OS Regional Office in their area.   With a few exceptions, large scale coverage of the urban areas was reported as being up to date for 1974.   Those authorities with responsibilities for rural areas, e.g. Gwent and Norfolk, expressed concern over the lack of availability of recent maps at medium and large scales.

5.4   The range of scales available was generally felt to be very good, and local authorities seem to make extensive use of maps at 1:1250, 1:2500, 1:10,000, 1:25,000 and 1:50,000.   One authority made a plea for more up to date mapping at the 1:25,000 scale, which was particularly useful in illustrating various distributions.   Hope was also expressed that new sheets in the 1:10,000 series would resolve the problem of the out of dateness of the previous mapping at 6" to the mile in rural areas.   Generally, however, there was no call for the production of maps at intermediate scales to those published.

5.5   Several authorities, e.g. Hampshire. Cheshire and Birmingham, expressed great interest in the OS digital mapping programme under which large scale plans in the 1:1250 and 1:2500 series are prepared by computer.   Cheshire and Birmingham both expressed the desire to utilise the digital maps for their areas as part of their own system.   Hampshire reported that they had done a study of the utility of the OS digital tapes to them.   Some authorities expressed concern over the available coverage of digital tapes.   They pointed out that at current rates of production it will be many years before a digital base will be complete for the whole area of a local authority. This was one of the conclusions of the Hampshire study.   They also noted that, whereas their computer was sufficiently powerful to handle Ordnance Survey digital material, the overall cost of doing so, and of the peripheral equipment and human resources involved, would need careful balancing against the benefits to be derived. For example, the local authorities consulted stated that there seemed little need to produce maps at different scales from those currently produced, and thought it relatively unlikely that the digital tapes will replace the published map as a base map for general local authority work in the near future.   All seemed agreed about the long term potential, but in the short term there are clearly many problems to be overcome if this new product is to be not only useful but economic for land use mapping in local authorities.

5.6   The Ordnance Survey's data restructuring project is at an early stage and no definitive report on it is published at the time of writing.   A full discussion of this issue is in any event beyond the scope of this project.   However, the Ordnance Survey have been good enough to furnish the following information.

> "The restructuring project will alter the data structure of the Ordnance Survey tapes into a form suitable for manipulation and this restructured data will be available to those who wish to manipulate it themselves. The system also includes a User Language (Land) to enable users to extract land parcels automatically with minimum human intervention.   The concept of a User Language is to provide users with a ready made means of manipulating the restructured data and providing the information requested on magnetic tape, formatted for input to specified computer hardware. It is envisaged that extracted information, including land parcel data, will be incorporated into a users information system, which could include appropriate land use information.
>
> The present restructuring project, which will provide the software to restructure all the data on the available Ordnance Survey tapes and provide a User Language (Land) will culminate in user trials ending in March 1977.
>
> It is envisaged that the restructuring software could be made available to those local authorities and other users in the future, who request it.   For this reason, specific attention has been paid to the portability of the software.   Whether or not the users have the restructuring software, they will have to provide computer resources to integrate the OS information into their own information systems. "

5.7   The Ordnance Survey also add that

> "Resulting from consultations with public and local authority users during 1975, the Ordnance Survey has now produced a general purpose plot programme which will overcome the early difficulties that had been experienced. "

5.8   So far as the applicability to land use mapping is concerned, both Cheshire and Birmingham indicated that the Ordnance Survey tapes in their cartographic format contain topographic onformation and do not include comprehensive land use data, even at the first order code level.   Local authorities cannot, therefore, expect to use them for the extraction and manipulation of land use information, for which additional data would have to be included.   Cheshire wrote to LAMSAC suggesting that prime land use classification should be included on the digital base being produced by the Ordnance Survey, and this subject is clearly one for further discussion, especially when local authorities have more experience of restructured Ordnance Survey information and the computer overheads involved in manipulating it. The extraction of particular feature codes and the measurement of, e.g. size of buildings, from digital tapes in conjunction with the use of point in polygon programs has many interesting possibilities. At the same time, it is possible to represent large amounts of land use information as computer-produced overlays to existing Ordnance Survey base maps. This relatively unsophisticated and economical technique is illustrated in Appendix I of this report.

6.   Geocoding

6.1   Every local authority visited during this project was concerned with geocoding - i.e. with the desirability of using a unique method of locational referencing in order easily to index and inter-relate many of the sets of data used for management. In 1972 DOE published their report General Information Systems for Planning (GISP): subsequently they have been concerned with a number of related projects such as the National Gazetteer Pilot Project, which has been actively concerned with the problem of "point referencing".

6.2   Detailed comment on progress in this important field is largely outside the scope of this report. But the subject has a direct association with mapping, and particularly with computer mapping. The National Grid is the obvious basis for a geocoding system and - unlike the situation in many other countries - is precisely printed on Ordnance Survey maps. The process of reading off grid references - typically for a centroid for every hereditament - is, however, extremely slow and somewhat error prone by manual methods. An improvement in speed and accuracy can be achieved by using semi-automatic digitising equipment which can provide results in computer-compatible form for merging, e.g. with the equivalent postal address. However, such equipment is expensive (c. £15,000 for one installation) and the reliability of results again depends on checking procedures, which themselves require concentrated and detailed human effort.

6.3   In this connection we record that in every local authority visited there were considerable quantities of data relating to land in terms of Ordnance Survey grid references (some in 6-figure, some even in 12-figure terms): some of this data was in manuscript form, some of it in digital form. However, we must also record our view that few authorities had effective accuracy and quality control of such grid reference data, and some had only cursory checking. Awareness of this aspect was drawn to our attention by Hampshire, who had to recode a file completely because the accuracy of grid reference data was not adequate.

7.   Management Information Systems

7.1   "Geocoding" in one form or another seems implicit in the various computer-based systems that are under development in order to speed and rationalise management decisions in local authorities. We noted several approaches of this kind that were relevant to land use mapping, and local authorities in our sample who are pursuing this theoretical solution are Newcastle, Coventry, Manchester and Leeds.

7.2   The basic unit on which information is collected by Newcastle is the parcel, which is the heart of the Planning Master Index.   The Planning Master Index has a record of approximately 120, 000 properties and parcels of land in Newcastle.   The visual centroid of each of these properties has been digitised and for each property the following information has been recorded: Address, National Grid co-ordinate, housing rent number, rate assessment number, postal code, floor number, floor space (new developments only), compulsory purchase orders and clearance areas and land uses. The index is at implementation stage but is not yet complete. Reorganisation has meant that properties in the new area added to the District have had to be incorporated.

7.3   Coventry is computerising land and property data as part of the Coventry Management Information System (CMIS). The land and property file of this system developed out of the earlier point data system.   The Point Data System began in 1969, and by July 1970 a gazetteer had been established containing all of Coventry's 120, 000 properties.   A geocode of the visual centroid of each property was digitised, with the use of a 12-figure grid reference, allowing the location of a property within one metre.   The Point Data System was never fully implemented, and on the incorporation of elements of the system into CMIS the property code was modified. The geocode was retained within the system, but its function is solely that of a locational reference · an attribute rather than a key. The property code is now the key reference of the system and this is a nine-digit code giving street code, property number and property division.

7.4   Manchester as part of its Management Information System is developing a Property Directory.   This will include addresses plus 12-figure National Grid references and a series of other references, e.g. rate assessment number and planning land use number.   The aim is to use this to co-ordinate information from a variety of individual files.   Digitised centroids are said now to have been attached to all numbered properties.

7.5 Leeds is building a comprehensive land and property data base as part of LAMIS (Local Authority Management Information System). The main linking agent is the UPRN (Unique Property Reference Number), which is a comprehensive 13-digit code. Leeds has also completed digitising all 350, 000 properties in the District. Both boundaries and centroids are digitised from OS maps at 1:1250 and 1:2500.

7.6 The integrated approach outlined above is a viable one, but is undeniably expensive, slow and technically and administratively difficult. None of these systems has been fully implemented, and even when the implementation stage is complete there will still be major operational problems. Output is largely tabular and statistical in form, although LAMIS is giving active consideration to graphical output. In the light of existing circumstances few local authorities will have the resources to emulate this approach in the near future. A DOE study is currently under way on the feasibility of operating LAMIS in other authorities.

8. Planning permissions

8.1 A somewhat simpler and more limited approach lies in the development of a computerised system for planning permissions. All local authorities visited are collecting information on approved planning applications, and this includes land use change by major categories. Several authorities indicated that, had there not been a statutory requirement for this data, it is unlikely that systems to collect and process it would have been set up so quickly, but none questioned seriously the value of having such data.

8.2 Once such files are established, updating by incorporation of approved planning applications is relatively easy, but getting data on when approved changes are actually implemented seems more problematical. This is partly due to the fact that the approval of applications is the responsibility of planning departments, whereas data on when proposed changes are actually made is collected by other departments. Consequently, in many authorities surveyed, reliable and total information was available only on planning permission for land use change rather than on the occurrence of real change on the ground.

8.3 Thirteen of the authorities surveyed were developing systems to record planning applications, and with locational references. However, only five of these (see paragraph 3.1) had completed basic land use surveys with which such changes could be compared. The previous land use of a parcel for which permission had been requested was stated in the application, but if no such request had been made the land use of a parcel was rarely known.

9.   Linkage of transport and land use data

In none of the approaches outlined above has the problem of
linking "flow" data to a locational reference been mentioned.
Transportation and activities relating to it are an important
land use, yet often transportation and planning studies are not
as closely related within a local authority as they might be.
Data on land can be linked to segments as well as to points or
areas, and segment referenced systems can deal with transportation data in a way which other locational referencing systems
cannot.   In Merseyside a pilot project on segment referencing
is under way, where an attempt is being made to link transportation and planning data.   The potential of linking land use
information to networks should not be ignored.

10.   Other sources of land use data, and the Rating File in particular

10.1   Co-ordination and even basic knowledge of data held within a local
authority is often difficult.   A DOE study on Information Availability
within two local authorities is currently under way and should
provide interesting results.   Local authorities are of course aware
that data on land are held by several depeartments within the
authority and that they are often not readily or quickly available.
Some authorities, e.g. Norfolk, have set up co-ordinating
structures to increase the availability of such data.   Our survey
has revealed that much basic data relating to land are held on maps,
often in manuscript form.   Coventry carried out a survey in 1971
and discovered that information in map form was held on:
Compulsory Purchase Orders, Comprehensive Development Areas,
Appropriation Plans, Lease Plans, Street Closures, General Plans
and a variety of miscellaneous "one-of-a-kind" topics.   Had the
survey been extended to all departments, the list would probably
have been much longer.   Surveys such as that carried out by
Coventry are unusual;   whereas the availability of data held in
numerical form is often known, the very existence of data in map
form is too often known only to a few people.   In one authority
officials in one department were utilising a small scale map of
land potential, indicating that they had written to many sources,
without success, to obtain the data from which the map had been
produced: it subsequently emerged that that data on which the
map was based had been separately collected and illustrated in
manuscript form on 1:1250 base maps by another department
within the same authority.

10.2   This kind of problem is often compounded when one looks at regional and national sources outside the local authorities. There is clearly a variety of information related to land use being collected by government departments, public utilities and public and private organisations of all kinds.   No comprehensive and regularly revised list of these sources exists, and much is therefore missed.   Even when local authorities are aware of such sources, information is not always available in a form, or with the timeliness, that is required.

10.3   Many officials expressed the opinion that it was often easier, and certainly faster, to go out and collect the information by survey than to obtain it from some other organisations.   Ad hoc operations of this kind may have much to recommend them where the nature of the enquiry is limited, geographically or in subject terms.   But on a wider or longer term basis the "go-out-and-look" technique can become uneconomic and inconsistent;   and, in the case of land use in particular, reference has already been made to the high costs of ad hoc surveys, which seem to have operated as a deterrent to making them at all.

10.4   Air photographs.   All authorities were well aware of the usefulness of air photographs, and often had commissioned photography ad hoc. Relatively little use of such material seemed made for direct land use planning purposes, although Merseyside used air photographs and marked on them (manually) the location of planning applications. Hampshire were also well aware of their potential, and supplied a photograph of Central Winchester which has been used as an alternative to the Ordnance Survey 1:10,560 base map in Appendix I (see item 6).   All work with air photographs that was noted in the authorities was on a manual basis and did not involve any aspects of computer interpretation or plotting: in this sense the photograph was generally - and reasonably - regarded as a "given object" rather similar to a printed map.

10.5   In other parts of the world the air photograph, and more recently the satellite image, has seemed to achieve a greater relative importance, particularly under circumstances where it is virtually the only detailed information about a site.   In Britain, however, a mass of supplementary information does exist, and often about subjects which cannot easily be interpreted from photography, e.g the detailed use of a property.   Even where it is possible to gather such detailed information from air photographs, the costs of doing so are comparable with the costs of ad hoc field survey. Even the use of photography as a means of frequent updating of land use patterns has limitations that may be imposed by, e.g. partial cloud cover at the time of the sortie.   Some of these matters are susceptible to improvement from the new techniques of remote sensing and the automatic analysis of the data recorded at different wave bands. The monitoring of land use patterns in, e.g. California from Landsat imagery has made interesting progress, and doubtless these techniques will be more widely used in Britain in the 1980s. Reference must also be made to a DOE project in which some five main urban land use categories have been plotted from air photography (dated 1969) on to 1:50,000 maps and are being digitised so that areas can be measured and changes in urban land use patterns can be monitored. This interesting project, however, is aimed at the sphere of national and regional strategy, and cannot be expected to provide detailed and large scale land use information.

10.6   An approach that, surprisingly, was not being used by any of the local authorities in this project, was to use the Rating File as a source of land use data. The Rating File, however, was the only computer file containing land use information on properties which was actually running and regularly updated in all the authorities in the survey.

10.7   The type of information held in the Rating File is in the form of property descriptions, and these are in terms as used by the Valuation Officer, not by the planner. Such files, like many others, also suffer from a lack of an effective locational reference or geocode other than street address. However, none of these problems seems insurmountable. Rates are essential to the income of all local authorities, and clearly the file dealing with them also has potential as a basic source of data for land use mapping. The data on these files might not give the optimal solution of total inter-relatedness of all data relating to land, nor would the land use categories be exactly those of the National Land Use Classification, but clean digital data about every hereditament, updated on a regular basis for all local authorities, does appear to be available from them. The potential of this approach is more fully examined later in this report and in the two Appendices.

11.   Mapping Systems in Use

11.1   In section 3 we have pointed to the absence of land use mapping, despite the use made of Ordnance Survey materials (section 4) and the interest in Geocoding and in Management Information Systems (5 and 6). At the same time, the need to inter-relate activities and uses of land as part of the planning process was acknowledged in all the authorities we visited; and, to this end, there was some evidence of overlay and "sieve mapping" techniques.

11.2   <u>The East Lothian System</u>.   The simple manual system used by
this authority gives some indication of cartographic potential.
The development of this system began in 1971 and initially there
was considerable involvement on the part of the Procedures and
Methods Group of the Scottish Development Department.   The
purpose of the system is to provide a basis for the collation of
information relating to development control.   The District is
covered by a series of maps on transparencies.   For
convenience of filing and use these are of A4 size and are kept
in loose-leaf binders.   The District is covered by 5 km squares
at 1:25, 000 with $\frac{1}{2}$ and $\frac{1}{4}$ km squares at 1:2, 500 for the towns.
Three transparencies are at the core of the system; a base map
showing transportation, a zoning map, and a control and projects
map.   Any drawing relating to the area or part of it can be added
to the system if it is portrayed on base maps at one of the "nested"
OS scales.   The Coal Board produces maps on OS bases of areas
in danger of subsidence.   These are simply photographed to
produce acetate overlays, and added to the file.   As material is
already on a transparent base, the inter-relationship between
significant variables can be demonstrated.   When a development
application is received, it is drawn up on tracing paper and, by
using an overhead projector, a decision-making body can immediately
see the relationship of the application to zoning and other constraints.
The application itself can easily be reproduced, as can many other
of the bases, by dyeline, for consultation with other departments and
outside agencies.   This overlay system has no computer involvement -
but it clearly could.   In more complex areas, where there is need
for scale flexibility, for fast analytical mapping of selected variables,
or for the precise measurement of areas, a computerised version
of this overlay system would appear to be a valuable enhancement.
The possibilities of this are implicit in the sample maps in
Appendix I.

11.3   <u>Computer mapping programs</u>.   The main program of which local
authorities had knowledge was SYMAP, the program being available
in eleven of the fifteen authorities visited.   Merseyside was the
only authority using SYMAP for anything other than the display of
census variables, extensive use of the program being made by the
Environmental Quality Group.   In two authorities the program was
available but not used at all, and of the others only Mid Glamorgan
and Hampshire were using SYMAP in anything other than a
minimal way.

11.4   None of the versions of SYMAP available to the local authorities
we visited had the full capabilities of the program available.   Most
had only the conformant option, with few of the numerous analytical
capabilities or the proximal or contour options.   In this respect the
program was rarely used at more than a third of its existing and
demonstrated potential.   Only in Merseyside was the graphic quality

in output even close to being acceptable, and in some authorities mention was made of the fact that the maps themselves were not widely accepted at committee. Line printer maps are crude, but judicious selection of print symbols together with photo-reduction and cartographic enhancement can much improve them. The standard line printer symbol is rectangular, not square, thus making the overlay of SYMAPs on OS base maps impossible. It is, however, not technically difficult to produce square print symbols. Even the simple step of printing on the blank reverse side of lined computer paper leads to considerable improvement in graphic quality. Coventry was the best example of an authority which had used SYMAP to produce rough maps which had then been manually redrawn for colour reproduction of a recent (1975) report. Such maps have also been used in a wide range of policy reports for Merseyside. SYMAP is more appropriate for handling census data than for the mass of detailed point data involved in mapping from Rating or Planning Application files. Examples of some of the alternative versions of SYMAP are illustrated in Appendix I.

11.5   Of other computer mapping programs, there was mention of BRADMAP in Leeds and of CAMAP in Edinburgh. During the visits to local authorities there seemed little knowledge of Linmap or Colmap, the two computer mapping programs developed by the DOE. The system is now available for use by local authorities on a bureau-type basis through the DOE, and is also on sale as a complete package. An example of Linmap is illustrated in Appendix I.

11.6   Grid square maps, while potentially illuminating - especially to their authors - seem to some users a compromise between statistics and "real maps", and depend on the availability of line printers - and the non-availability of plotters - in many local authority computer installations. We believe that this balance may change and that more computer graphic facilities will become available. Indeed, a number of the authorities visited already had drum plotters, and under these circumstances a program like GIMMS is an alternative method of representing statistical surfaces (see Appendix I). The program was developed in Edinburgh University, although it was not actually in use in any of the authorities visited.

11.7   Several authorities, e.g. Norfolk, Cheshire and Hampshire, showed interest in more advanced forms of computer graphics and in the possibilities of interactive work with cathode ray tubes in which a "dialogue" with the map data base takes place. During the next decade many developments on these lines may find them-selves translated from research environments into operational tools in British local authorities.

11.8   One requirement for such future development - emphasised by Cheshire - is for software that is, on the one hand, robust and transparent, and, on the other hand, is not so personalised that others in a department have difficulty in operating it when the original inventor has moved elsewhere.

12.   <u>Experimental mapping</u>

12.1   Despite the absence of land use mapping, it was evident from our study that the ability to handle land use information was accepted as a generally desirable end by local authorities. This was especially so when based on data that were

(a) regularly/frequently revised;

(b) fast and cheap to handle;

(c) allowed of analysis and quantification;

(d) geographically complete and detailed.

12.2   Given these four criteria for land use information, some will prefer to study it in statistics, others in maps, and many in both. It follows that if map making is slow, expensive and inflexible there will be some prejudice against it.

12.3   Computer cartography has a significant role to play here in that flexibility, accuracy and speed can now be brought to the thematic overlay technique. The survey revealed an almost total lack of awareness of this potential. It was with this in mind that the ECU experimented with some sample mapping of data from local authorities.

12.4   Data suitable for such an experiment were discussed with local authorities during the survey. Some lead in this matter was taken by Hampshire, who were at that time studying the shopping pattern in central Winchester. Norfolk were also keen to experiment with data about local bus services in rural regions, and the associated factors of population characteristics, car ownership and provision of shops. Doubtless, it would have been possible to identify other equally interesting and real problems in each of our sample of local authorities. It was, however, important to generalise and to establish whether one reasonably typical land use mapping problem was susceptible to similar treatment in a number of different authorities; thus in general the sample maps concentrate on the distribution of commercial properties. The need to establish whether the same kind of treatment would apply to different authorities had another consequence - that of limiting rather severely the area of each sample. This reason also limited the actual samples of map output to seven out of the twelve authorities who furnished data (all of which was in fact prepared and digitised, but some of which was patently repetitive in nature).

It will be appreciated that constraints of time and resources have made most of the maps no more than samples of methods and not of any intrinsic merit as statements of land use in different places. But clearly there are few problems in applying the methodologies more widely.

12.5   In concentrating mainly on commercial premises, the sample maps have in the main been derived from two principal sources:

(a)   Planning Permissions;

(b)   Rating File.

Inevitably the planning file is not concerned with all properties, but only with those for which planning permission is sought. The Rating File, by contrast, deals with all rated properties.

12.6   Most of the maps in the Appendix are based on the overlay principal, and assume a standard Ordnance Survey base map (usually printed in buff) as a background to the special information. The point that actual overlay transparencies, rather than the use of two-colour printing, might well be used in practice will be obvious: such matters depend largely on whether the information is to be published and distributed or is to be discussed more informally.

12.7   Some of the map samples were seen by some of the local authorities during the course of the project. Interest was expressed in the capability that the maps demonstrated so far as sources of information, speed of handling and economy of graphics were concerned.

12.8   The comments on each of the maps in the Appendix describe the stages of this small computer mapping operation and the times involved. Doubtless, the application of such processes on a more regular or more massive basis would lead to economies of effort. It will be noted, for example, that nearly twice as much time has been involved in this experiment in the manual/editorial stages of extracting, compiling and checking data as in the automated stages of digitising, processing and plotting. At the same time, the potential for making many additional or alternative plots from such a data base, at different scales, of different groupings, in different symbols, is as considerable as it is quick and cheap.

12.9   The majority of maps in Appendix I are produced in the ECU by equipment that are not widely available within authorities at present. However, examples of drum plotter maps and of line printer maps produced (from data tapes supplied by Hampshire) outside ECU by more standard computing equipment have also been included.

13.   Costs of land use mapping

13.1   In all authorities visited the cost factor loomed large.   During
the survey (1975) it was evident that the "no growth" financial
situation made new developments difficult, e.g. in collecting land
use information: even the maintenance of current levels of
development was not easy.   Cost effectiveness needs to be
convincingly demonstrated if changes in procedure are to be
implemented.   That said, it proved to be extremely difficult to
assess the current costs of land use data collection and their
subsequent use.   One of the major components in this work is
staff costs, and these are broken down by department.   Furthermore, cost factors vary with the size of the authority and the way
in which different authorities administer different taks.   Thus,
for example, Lambeth and Birmingham have full-time teams
working on the collection and up-dating of land use information,
but this situation is not true in the majority of authorities.   In
most authorities the initial high cost of installing a computer
system has generally been related to some specific task such as
rate demands, and the associated accounting and computer time
for other purposes is often not charged back to the task concerned.
Under these circumstances we were forced to conclude that
meaningful generalisations about cost could not be made.

13.2   Where local authorities have become involved in handling locational
data in quantities that demand computer help, they have been faced
with a choice between purchasing equipment such as digitising
tables and training their own staff to do the job, or subcontracting
the work to a bureau.   It may be useful to record that bureau
charges (1976) for digitising point data are of the order of £0.15
per point, and this includes attaching two feature codes to each
point and a check of all digitised locations.   Thus a total of around
£15,000 would be involved for an authority with 100,000
hereditaments, and for a basic operation that would not require
repeating in toto but would require some regular updating.   This
figure is roughly comparable with the capital cost of buying a
digitising table and peripheral equipment, but developing software,
training staff and carrying out the digitising and checking it are
sometimes substantial additions.   We observed that a few local
authorities had purchased their own equipment, others had used
bureaux, and some had kept clear of digitised locational data.
Given that land use data is available from some other source with
locations in digital form, the costs of handling it statistically and
cartographically are greatly reduced.   Under manual conditions
the final drawing of a map may be more lengthy/costly than its
compilation: under computer conditions the actual process of map
output can become very fast and equivalently cheap.   So the crux
of the matter lies in identifying a source of land use data which is
already in digital form.

14.   Sources of land use data: the potential of the Valuation Lists

14. 1   Before any land use map can be prepared, either by traditional or
by automated means, data on land use, which is regularly updated,
must be available. It was clear from our survey that land use
data collection, as a separate item, was not the highest priority
for local authorities, and, largely because of the cost factor at a
time of extreme financial stringency, it often remained undone.

14. 2   In such a stringent financial atmosphere the notion of instigating
efficient new land use surveys or of speeding up such on-going land
use surveys as do exist is not likely to make much progress. Of
course it is true that Britain has a rich diversity of surveys; but
many of these are not primarily about the land but about population
characteristics or particular industries or trades or medical
conditions. Most, if not all, of these are of a statutory nature and
are of importance to local authority planners, especially in drafting
structure plans. The Census of Population is especially so, despite
its ten-year periodicity; nevertheless, the smallest spatial unit -
parish or ward - in terms of which the Census is published, or the
enumeration district in terms of which it is collected, represent
a much coarser geographical network than the hereditament, which
is often the real basis of land use. The Building Completions file
and the Health Inspections file are "location specific" but of
necessity do not deal with all locations. The Valuation List
prepared by the Inland Revenue (and the Rating files of the local
authorities which are often derived from it) is a survey that
specifies individual rated hereditaments, and which does seem to
offer possibilities for land use mapping. Since information about
the rateable value of each hereditament is publicly available and
is combined with information about use, the planner seems to have
at hand a ready-made source of "free" data in quantified form.

14. 3   In preparing the map section of the report and at the Workshop in
February 1976, this approach was discussed with the local
authority representatives. Information about Rating files had
not been collected during the survey stage of the project, as rating
is not a concern of planning departments. It became clear that
some of the planners were not aware that land use information
could be derived from Rating files, and that none of them was using
this source: this seems to be partly because the Rating files are
held at District level and differing degrees of detail are extracted
from the Valuation List, as required for District purposes.

14.4   In May 1976 the Layfield Committee on Local Government Finance
        reported.   Some of its proposals affect the Valuation Lists, and
        hence the future potential of Rating files.   (At the time of writing
        no decision has been taken by the Government as to the extent to
        which they accept these proposals).   As a result ECU held
        discussions with the Valuation Office ADP Feasibility Study Team
        (June 1976).   The following notes and the detailed comparison of
        the categories in the Valuation List with those of the National Land
        Use Classification (Appendix II) are based on these talks.

14.5   The local authority rating files are in essence the machinery for
        collecting the rates by means of which local authorities finance the
        major part of their expenditure.   Rating is therefore central to
        local government in Britain.   The Layfield Committee has summed
        this up well (para 2,143):

        "As a result of continuous developments over more
        than three and a half centuries, rating has become
        deeply embedded in the taxation and local government
        systems.   There exists a substantial administrative
        apparatus for assessing, levying and collecting rates.
        There is a large body of professional and lay staff
        experienced in rating in local authorities and the
        government, as well as in many large industrial and
        commercial undertakings and in private practice."

14.6   Rating files for local authorities in England and Wales are derived
        from the Inland Revenue's Valuation List.   This statutory document
        is the responsibility of central government and thus achieves
        comparability between local authorities.   In England and Wales the
        lists are prepared by Inland Revenue Valuation Officers and held by
        the rating authority, generally at District Council offices and as a
        public document.   In Scotland the system is very similar, except
        that the Assessors are appointed and controlled by the local
        authority.

14.7   The value of property has a direct relationship to its use.   Hence
        the full Valuation List incorporates a detailed description of the use
        of each property.   The Valuation Office, as a precursor to possible
        computer developments, is (1976) developing a hierarchical
        classification of the descriptions of use that have in past years been
        used by their Valuation Officers.   This classification assumes some
        1200 different uses, and some examples are shown in Appendix II.
        The List is, however, in course of development and the final version
        may differ in detail.   It should be noted, however, that when the
        Rating File is generated by the local authority the detailed descriptions
        of uses are often condensed.   Sometimes the local authority has
        decided to keep quite a lot of these detailed categories - e.g. one
        District in Hampshire retained 250 use codes in their file;
        sometimes the information is condensed right down to the 50 or so

categories required by the "Statistical Analysis of numbers and rateable values of all hereditaments assessed in the Valuation List" (known as CV/R/140 and also illustrated in Appendix II). At least, all authorities themselves hold information about use of all hereditaments in these categories: and with this information on use is, of course, information on value.

14. 8   The work of updating the Valuation List is a continuous process and the local authority is directed to update the list on approximately a monthly basis.   This updating of old valuations does enable change of use to be picked up very quickly; however, the valuation figures are liable to grow increasingly out of date until a general Revaluation takes place.   These Revaluations are planned to be on a five-yearly basis, though in practice they are less frequent than that: the Layfield Report has urged that there should be a Revaluation in 1980.

14. 9   Granted the importance of the Rating File to the running of any local authority, it was not surprising to find that all authorities in our sample had at least some information about rates on a computer file.   At the same time, much of the detailed description was often in manual files.

15.   Shortcomings of the Valuation List as a source of land use information

15. 1   One shortcoming of the Valuation Lists as a direct source of land use mapping is that the data in them is not geocoded.   A recent (1974/5) study on introducing property reference numbers for each hereditament was carried out by the Valuation Office, who worked closely with the National Gazetteer Pilot Study in this context.   As a result, the Valuation Office propose to adopt a Property Reference Number (VOPREN) for any system they may institute.   This number codifies the full postal address, but is not a location code that would allow direct computer mapping.   The use of various alternative systems of providing geographical locations, including postal codes, was considered.   The methods of adding geocodes used in the field trials added a significant extra expense for an organisation not primarily concerned with maps.

15. 2   While it is true that the Valuation Office has little direct interest in land use mapping, the issue of geocoding the Valuation Lists becomes proportionately more important in relation to the useful- ness of the information for local authority land use mapping. Furthermore, Layfield comments that regional variations in valuations - both throughout the country and within the same area or town - are of some significance (para 14. 148 and 35. 156). The mapping of valuation or rating data seems to be a useful way of illustrating and monitoring this.

15.3   So it may be appropriate to re-examine the possibilities of providing the Valuation List or the Rating files with codes that will enable maps to be derived quickly, effectively and cheaply from them. There seem several possible approaches to this task which could be carried out by local authorities, should it remain impractical for the Valuation Office to incorporate such codes in their Valuation Lists.

15.4   The first of these approaches might be called "selective geocoding" - as opposed to "saturation geocoding" - in effect it was the approach applied in preparing the sample maps in this report. It consisted of selecting topics - or land use categories - of particular interest from each Rating file (mostly shops and offices), identifying these by pinning down their addresses on a large scale map, and then digitising them. In practice this involved handling some 10% of all the hereditaments in any of the sampled areas. Clearly it would be possible to use various criteria for picking a sample from the Valuation List: probability of change of use might be one, major value another. Furthermore, the process could be cumulative, e.g. in year 1 shops of over certain values could be geocoded and added to the file; in year 2 offices could be added, and so on. A gradual approach of this kind may also have practical advantages from the computer processing standpoint: certainly there are dangers in aiming at theoretical"completeness" in data bases and hence loading files with an overburden of additional data when, in fact, the major part of such data may never be used.

15.5   A second approach may lie through a combination of the selective geocoding of points and the allocation of street segment codes (or block frontage codes) as used in traffic censuses, etc. In this approach the geocodes would aim to pinpoint the conspicuous or significant building or location, while the street segments would generalise the background pattern, e.g. in residential areas, bearing some relation to the U.S. 'DIME' system. This approach would require further development through a project.

15.6   A third possibility exists for those authorities (e.g. Leeds, Coventry, Birmingham, Manchester and Newcastle in our sample) who have built up a list of geocodes - but they are a minority. This lies in using a computer address matching system and linking the address plus geocode and the equivalent addresses without a geocode in the Valuation List. An address matching experiment is currently being carried out by Hampshire; this is on the lines of FRANSTAN as developed in Marseilles. A related technique of matching UPRN plus geocode and equivalent VOPREN (see 15.1) without a geocode, could be adopted in the future. Note also that some authorities, e.g. Liverpool, having attached point references to each property, are not making extensive use of the data in that form: linked to Valuation List data they would seem to have a ready-made source of computer land use maps.

15. 7   A second shortcoming of the Valuation List for land use mapping lies in its different definitions of "use" as against the National Land Use Classification. These differences naturally reflect important differences of approach as between Valuation Officers and Planners. However, it must be noted that most authorities studied were not in fact using the full classification proposed by NLUC. Details of correspondences - and lack of them - will be evident from a study of Appendix II, but it is clear that a substantial correspondence can be found, and this covers a high proportion of the total number of hereditaments involved (e. g. 21 million for England and Wales). Lack of correspondence lies mainly in the treatment of industrial properties, where NLUC takes account of the taxonomy of the Standard Industrial Classification; but the Valuation Office may, on developing their classification, meet this point. However, industrial properties account for only 0. 5% of all hereditaments in England and Wales. While the classification of land use in the Valuation Lists may not be exactly what planners would like in an ideal world, the fact that these classifications are associated with values gives them the great merit of being quantifiable. Furthermore, they do exist and are regularly updated.

15. 8   It should also be noted that many planning authorities are using their own classifications: some of these are very close in detail to the NLUC; others are not. Most are compatible at the highest order level. But even within planning departments of local authorities in our sample, a dichotomy of approach to classification seemed to exist, the requirements of development control often having some particular idiosyncracies.

16.   <u>Significance of Layfield Committee's proposals</u>

Our survey indicated to us that land use mapping stood in great need of a substantial cornerstone of information - of a data base. This the Valuation List appears to provide. Three of the proposals of the Layfield Committee are likely - if adopted - to make this source of information even more valuable for planners - i. e.

(a)   Regular revaluation every five years or less.

(b)   Valuation to be on the basis of capital value so far as domestic property is concerned.

(c)   Inclusion of Crown Lands and agricultural property in the system.

If required by Government to carry out a revaluation by the early 1980s, the Valuation Office will doubtless be under pressure to establish any new procedures as quickly as possible. If their data is to provide the basis for some renaissance in land use mapping, there may be little time for delay in optimising the ways and means of handling it.

17.   Summary

17.1   The ECU was asked to assess the current and potential need for
land use data in local authorities; and whether these needs were
for handling such information by conventional or automated means,
and in cartographic or tabular form.

17.2   An assumption existed that the traditional practice of land use
mapping - especially in towns -was a standard procedure among
local authority planners.   Our survey showed this to be misleadingly
optimistic: it revealed that the traditional land use map was rarely
being used in the planning process - or elsewhere.

17.3   In so far as it is true that land use mapping is a low priority task,
the main reason for its demise appears to lie in the high costs of
collecting the data on a basis that is both sufficiently frequent and
sufficiently detailed.

17.4   Planning departments of local authorities have substantial needs for
data about land, and these are often common to other departments.
Some duplication of effort in collecting such data seems liable to
ensue, and this has lead some authorities to co-ordinate available
information, e.g. through inter-departmental Intelligence Sections.

17.5   One of the sectors of local authority planning in which land use is
an important issue is in Development Control.   Virtually all
development demands a statement of the existing and of the
proposed future land use on the site concerned.   Many hundreds
of thousands of applications are handled by local authorities
annually.   Unhappily, the information that can be derived from
planning approvals is limited in value because it is not always
known whether the development requested has in fact been carried
out, i.e. whether the land use has changed or not.   Also, because
such approvals are generally treated individually, they give few
pointers to synoptic change in an area such as might be useful in
monitoring proposals advanced in a Structure Plan.   Development
control does, of course, provide some statistics relating to land
use change per annum, and this is a statutory requirement.

17.6   Other areas for which land use information is seen as being relevant
are for the preparation and monitoring of Structure Plans and in
connection with the Community Land Act and DOE statutory returns.

17.7   The survey noted a number of Management Information schemes
based on computers, and a growing awareness of the advantage
of holding locational data in the form of "geocodes".   Although many
of these schemes used maps as sources, the possibilities of
deriving maps as a form of output from such systems had made

little progress. Clearly also, many of the schemes themselves were still at an early, if not experimental, stage of development.

17.8 Where local authorities had simple computer mapping programs like SYMAP, they often did not use them.

17.9 The survey was discouraging about the level of awareness of the potential of the map, although there were some exceptions, such as East Lothian. This aspect may be related to the decline of traditional land use mapping, which is seen as expensive and slow to prepare; and once prepared, tended to be inflexible in use (e.g. requiring remaking for any change of scale). Furthermore, such traditional maps provided an unquantified picture at a time when quantification is in vogue.

17.10 In contrast to the land use and thematic mapping, the topographical map seems in as great demand as ever, and local authorities appreciated the good service that they obtain from the Ordnance Survey, especially in the considerable range of scales which makes them particularly suitable as base maps for the overlay of transparencies or the overprinting of special topics. Reaction to the digital version of the Ordnance Survey maps was naturally more uncertain, since local authorities have not yet had much experience of the technical problems of using such data, nor of the cost benefits that might follow. Although the digital version of the Ordnance Survey maps does not itself contain land use information, the restructuring software package is said to allow users to add their own land use data to the individual land parcels created during the restructuring process.

17.11 Some swing of interest towards the use of statistics in local authorities, while admirable in itself, seems to have deflected enthusiasm away from cartography, rather than towards it as the proper and natural counterpart of statistics. Doubtless, this is related to the ease with which almost all computers can produce listings and tabulations, and the difficulty that so many of them still have in producing even the crudest graphics. This we believe to be a temporary phase, and many general indicators point to a wide growth in computer graphics within the next decade. Such a trend is likely to be helpful to land use mapping if, and only if, it coincides with the availability of land use data in a format suitable for mapping.

17.12 A possible way out of the difficulties in data collection is to identify a surrogate for land use - a substitute for the ad hoc land use survey. The report suggests that the Valuation List of the Inland Revenue and the Rating Lists which are derived from it are worth serious examination in this context.

A detailed study of the possibilities was outside the terms of reference and resources of this project. Nevertheless, the Valuation List does deal with every hereditament and has a good updating system; it classifies hereditaments into 40 or so use categories, and there are plans to extend this hierarchically to some 1200 categories; it also provides a rateable value for each hereditament and hence offers a quantification of land parcels; it is publicly available; and a new revaluation of the country is currently being planned which may involve the holding of all data in a form ready for computer manipulation and printout. The proposals of the Layfield Committee are pertinent to the Valuation List and the Rating files, and if accepted seem likely to strengthen the value of the data for land use purposes. It should, however, be noted that, like many other sources of information, the Valuation List does not include grid references from which mapping by computer - or by hand - could instantly be derived. Further examination of methods of geocoding the Valuation List are suggested.

17.13   In a map section, data supplied by the local authority planning departments has been edited, digitised and plotted under the ECU system of computer cartography, and times for performing the operations are stated. The sample maps deal with seven different authorities in an attempt to illustrate a common handling procedure for quite different areas. In many of the sample maps information from Rating files has been used; in most cases the computer-derived information is overprinted in black on a standard Ordnance Survey base map in brown.

17.14   The map samples show a limited number of graphical treatments that can be applied to data about land use under the particular and relatively sophisticated system of computer cartography at ECU. Also included is an equivalent map made by a drum plotter of a type more likely to be available in local authorities, and several maps resulting from running the SYMAP, the GIMMS and the Linmap programs on census data. The point at issue is that, given the data in digital form, there is scope for quite new graphical possibilities in mapping, ranging from the fast ephemeral CRT display to complex multicolour cartography; indeed, for some purposes the cartographic data should be able to yield not maps but measurements of area or length of line. Some of this potential versatility depends upon the availability of specialised equipment within local authorities; as much depends on some freshness of approach to a traditional subject.

17.15   In the final analysis it is as difficult to prove or disprove the case for reintroducing cartography into land use management as it is to prove or disprove the effectiveness of the planning process. Nevertheless, it is reasonable to assert that spatial organisation of data in map form brings advantages that cannot be obtained from other methods. New cartographic techniques using the computer do enhance this potential, but the potential is not simply confined to computer technology - it has always been there.

18.   Conclusions

We see two clear conclusions:

A.   Data collection and revision is the key problem in land use.
        If data are available, then the technology to manipulate and
        present them can be brought into play.   If the data are not
        available, then the technology is of limited use.   This
        report emphasises that ad hoc collection of land use data is
        expensive.

B.   This report has made a strong case for using the Valuation
        List or Rating file for this purpose.   We have demonstrated
        that land use maps can be made from Rating files.   The
        opportunity to refine and add to these files will probably
        never be greater than it is now.   Our major proposal is that
        this potential be further examined on the lines of Appendix II,
        and also to see if properties could be geocoded during the
        revaluation process.   Delay is not practical as, given
        Layfield's proposals, the needs of the Inland Revenue are
        pressing.

EXPERIMENTAL MAPPING

EXPERIMENTAL MAPPING

(a)   This appendix is referred to in Section 11 of the main report.

(b)   To a large degree the set of maps in this appendix explains itself. Some notes about the work may, however, provide more detailed information about such matters as methods, timings, etc., which bear on the cost/effectiveness of making land use maps by computer.

(c)   Selection of sample maps. A request for data for sample mapping was sent to the local authorities concerned in the project. The suggested sample was to be the area of a single 1:1250 or 1:2500 map with the equivalent data for planning, rating and other files believed to be of interest. By a closing date of December 1975, twelve authorities had provided such data. All the data was then edited and digitised by ECU on the lines envisaged for this map section. Not surprisingly, some of this was repetitive, i.e. it showed no new facets of the problem; for some of it the sample areas selected happened to have little land use variation, e.g. suburban houses only. In the event, therefore, only the data sets of seven of the authorities were mapped. Note, however, that the examples cover England, Scotland and Wales; also a County Council, a District, a London Borough and a Metropolitan District. Most of the maps deal only with small areas, since the sample data related to the areas of single Ordnance Survey plans. However, one authority, Hampshire, provided data covering the central area of Winchester, and this extended over six plans at the 1:1250 scale: this larger area has illustrated mapping at different scales from a single cartographic data base. Smaller scale mapping has also been illustrated for the administrative District of Winchester (the former Rural District) and for part of a Rural District in Norfolk. At a final stage in this report DOE made Linmap available to local authorities and requested that an example of this system be included with the sample maps. The central area of Newcastle - Map 12 - is simply printed from reproduction material supplied by them; no comparable processing or production times are available (hence its omission from the table in paragraph (h)).

(d)   Form of the data. In almost every case the data was not supplied to ECU in digital form; it was supplied either in manuscript or as computer listings. This partly reflects the fact that most authorities - not unreasonably - assume their digital data is for internal, not external, computer processing, and that computer listings are the expected end product of their system. Furthermore, different computing systems exist within local authorities, and even when two authorities have the same systems they often use different formats, etc. Theoretically, of course, data on one computer can be read by another. In practice, however, this may require special translation, etc. (e.g. as between 7-track and 9-track magnetic tape), which in the case of this particular experiment would have taken more resources than the rest of the work put together and extended the elapsed time. So most of the maps are based on computer listings edited manually and put again into digital form in the ECU. In one case - census data for the District of Winchester - the information was mapped direct from a magnetic tape supplied by Hampshire (see items 9 and 10).

(e) The circumstances of this ECU experiment made a combination of manual and computerised methods sensible, quick and cheap, and such an arrangement is by no means to be despised on larger scale experiments. At some point, however, the costs of writing, testing and using software to translate data from an existing format into one suitable for mapping will break even.

(f) The graphics. The graphics used on the maps reflect the idiosyncracies of the medium used. Most of them are produced by the high accuracy plotter at the ECU, and the symbols etc. are designed to make economic use of that particular equipment. Attention is drawn to the black lines by which individual locations are shown and which can be repeated at a range of scales to give precise locations: however, these line symbols require that each location has to be digitised by two points - a street front position plus another point to provide the angle at which the property lies to the street. It is of course perfectly possible from these two digitised positions to select a single location if point symbols rather than line symbols are to be used: see item 8. (The extra time to provide the two points involved an increase of about 10% in digitising time, and under the circumstances of this experiment: note also that total digitising time was only about 17% of total time).

(g) The inclusion of maps made by drum plotter, by line printer and by tape-controlled photo-typesetter shows some alternative graphical possibilities from different equipment. At the same time, the handling of area patterns on items 4 and 5 shows some of the economic methods available within a high accuracy system such as the ECU one. The point of importance is the graphic versatility that is readily achieved, given a properly coded and edited data base. Special information of this kind can be rapidly overlaid on standard Ordnance Survey base maps.

(h) Stages of processing. The table shows the times spent in ECU in preparing the data for the maps. It must be emphasised that these times relate to the preparation of a data set from which a number of maps of different topics or groupings can be plotted. In fact, in the ECU system the final stage of plotting the maps takes place unattended and overnight and is not a "chargeable" or significant item. Generally the data sets related to an entire OS map and were thus often larger than the area selected in the map sample as printed here.

	1	2	3	4 & 5	6, 7 & 8	9 & 10	11	
	Dunbar	Pontypridd	Lambeth	Coventry	Winchester City	Winchester District	South Norfolk	% times
Select data from lists and compile sites/codes	4.00	2.30	7.00	7.30	16.00	-	8.00	42%
Check compilation	2.30	2.00	4.00	2.00	8.15	-	3.00	20%
Digitise	0.40	2.10	1.30	4.05	6.50	-	3.00	17%
Process by computer	0.30	1.00	1.00	1.15	1.30	-	1.30	6%
Check computer output	0.15	0.15	1.00	1.15	6.05	-	0.45	9%
Prepare/specify plot (plotting not logged)	0.20	1.00	0.15	0.45	3.00	-	1.00	6%
Total times (hours & minutes)	8.15	8.55	14.45	16.50	41.40[3]	40.00[1]	17.15	
No. of sites located x feature codes per site	78x3	178x5	205x6	31x3[2]	566x7		73x5[2]	

(1) The preparation stages for the Winchester Rural District maps - items 9 & 10 - are excluded, as they were not comparable: i.e. the Census data was already coded and available for direct input to the SYMAP and GIMMS programs from magnetic tape. However, total input preparation time was 40.00 hours (plus computer running time of 1.30 hours on a main frame machine). The eight maps reproduced here amounted to 8 man hours and .30 machine processing hours.

(2) Much of the work on Coventry and South Norfolk was the digitising and coding of boundaries and roads, etc., in contrast to the site digitising that was the principal element of the other examples.

(3) Winchester City data covered six sheets at 1:1250 scale.

NB: Map 12 - Newcastle - omitted from this table: see paragraph (c) above.

34

(j)   The editing processes are effectively illustrated by item 2 (Pontypridd), which shows the kinds of data that were selected, compiled, digitised and processed to produce computer versions of lists and a key map for final checking of the data base. The evidence of what is held on this small ECU file implies the range of maps that can be retrieved under such a system.

(k)   <u>The maps</u>

The numbers (1-12) each refer to a display consisting sometimes of a single map, sometimes of a group of maps.

Items 1 to 8 are overprinted direct on copies of Ordnance Survey maps. Boundaries on items 9, 10 and 11 are also digitised from Ordnance Survey sources. The material is reproduced by permission of the Director General, Ordnance Survey

1.   <u>East Lothian: Dunbar High Street</u>

The source of the two maps is the Scottish Assessors Roll, which is the equivalent of the English Rating File. One map shows <u>all</u> shops; the other uses categories of use to select four types of shop.

2.   <u>Mid Glamorgan: Central Pontypridd</u>

The map forms a key to the complete print out and illustrates the way in which much of the data for other maps is held in the system. An Ordnance Survey 1:1250 map sheet was selected and the rating and planning files were searched to locate commercial premises, which were then given key numbers on the map.

3.   <u>Lambeth: Streatham High Road</u>

The two maps of commercial premises are based on the rating file and on planning permissions (in this case from what is called the CLUSTER file). The rating file map shows three categories of premises and three floor levels for the activity. The planning file shows applications for change of use. Interesting differences between the two files appear at 3 Sunnyhill Road and 254 Streatham High Road, which are shown on the planning map but not on the rating one. This could well be explained by the fact that these are planning applications that have not yet been converted into actuality. (Inconsistencies throughout all the data sets involved in the experiments were uncommon).

Coventry: Eagle Street Action Area

4.   The land use patterns which underprint the Ordnance
      Survey base were derived from a multicoloured manuscript
      map from the planning office.   The patterns were digitised
      and the data encoded so that any land use category (or all of
      them) could be retrieved.   A small difference in shape can
      be seen on the junction of Stoney Stanton Road and Harnall
      Lane East, where road realignment has taken place.

5.   The second Coventry map shows undeveloped land,
      distinguishing public and private ownership; this information
      was derived from a manuscript planning map.   In addition to
      plotting the outlines of land concerned, the computer also
      measured the area of such undeveloped land on this map - a
      total of c. $4\frac{1}{4}$ hectares: equally, it could have measured the
      areas of any particular parcels.   This ability to measure
      any specified area - or, if need be, length of line - is a
      quantifying function that computer mapping can bring to the
      problems of land use.   Area measurement can in some cases
      be usefully combined with point-in-polygon searches within a
      data base, and these may sometimes be an alternative to
      cartography, although with their own costs and shortcomings.

Hampshire: Central Winchester

The sequence of 10 maps displayed in items 6, 7 and 8 show
some of the aspects of the set of data prepared for the largest
of these particular map experiments.   (It should, of course,
be noted that this sample is an extremely small data set in
any real planning terms).   The data has been derived from
the rating file and from the planning application file.

6.   The set of maps dealing with eight different topics provides an
      analytical picture of the information which might be difficult to
      obtain from statistics.   Two of the topics - planning
      permissions - are overlaid on air photographs.

7.   In the particular case of Central Winchester the scale of 1:2500
      seems well suited to displaying the rateable values of commercial
      premises - and to indicating floor levels.

8.   More detailed site-by-site matters of land use may call
      for a 1:1250 scale, and these two maps employ a range of point
      symbols over one particular "window" of a selected area.
      The information on the two maps is identical, but the symbols
      on the lefthand page are drawn by flat bed plotter, and those on
      the righthand page by drum plotter of a type available in some
      local authorities.

Hampshire: Winchester Rural District

Items 9 and 10 display Population Census information, as opposed to land use in the strict sense. They use the SYMAP and GIMMS programs.

9.   Three of the SYMAP examples deal with % population over retirement, and use three different versions of the program on the same data for the same area. It will be seen that each SYMAP also provides its legend with a frequency diagram. The ease and speed with which this program is able to produce maps in great quantities makes it vital to select most carefully what is to be undertaken, to avoid overwhelming users with indigestible numbers of maps. SYMAPS are not generally intended for exact fit over a precise base map, and some users have consequently classed them as diagrams rather than maps - a distinction that may not be of much consequence for planning purposes.

A very approximate scale of 1:200,000 can be applied to both 9 and 10.

10.   The GIMMS maps are each choropleths and they deal with three distributions (% students; retired; under five). A fourth composite map brings together three factors (% retired; > 1 per room; two cars). The maps are drawn on a drum plotter.

11.   ### Norfolk: South Norfolk Rural District

This pair of maps again handles information about parishes, and the 'wind-rose' symbols provide quantitative data, which may take a user a little time to comprehend fully. The second map combines four factors (bus services; car owners; shops; population change) for each parish, and shows the pattern of A roads in brown, with those stretches with less than daily bus service in black "filling" lines. Both maps were drawn on the ECU flat bed plotter, which scaled the 'wind-rose' arms from digital data for each parish.

12.   ### Newcastle

This map illustrates the Linmap technique, which has many features in common with SYMAP and GIMMS. The final map is produced either by a tape-controlled photo-typesetter, as here, or by a standard line printer.

———————————

EAST LOTHIAN
Dunbar – High Street

Shops – from the rating file

1

All shops ►

◄ Selected types of shops

||||| Shop, workshop & store
|||• Shop & tearoom
▌▌▌ Shop & bakery
█ Shop, cellar & warehouse

Scale 1:2500

Study area ►

2

**Mid Glamorgan
Central Pontypridd**

**Commercial premises—from
rating & planning files**

Key map

| Premise
alignment

|17 Reference
number

Scale 1:1250

KEY TO MAP

Computer Printout - for Reference or Checking

Columns (working from the left) show:

I System sequence number not on map

II-V Co-ordinates of start and end of locational lines (in digitiser units from SW corner)

VI Number of feature codes attached to each reference

VII Site reference number (as on map)

VIII One of four selected commercial premises categories derived from rating file. (1= shop; 2= office; 3= combined; 4= others)

IX One of seven sub-categories of shop derived from rating file. (1= house & shop; 2= shop; 3= shop & store; 4= shop & showroom; 5= shop & workshop; 6= shop, cafe & house; 7= no entry)

X One of six sub-categories of office derived from rating file. (1= office; 2= office & store; 3= office & house; 4= office & flat; 5= office & showroom; 7 or 9= no entry)

XI (NB: This entry is beneath first co-ordinate in column II). One of eight planning categories from planning permissions file. (1= new development; 2= alteration; 3= conversion; 4= extension; 5= change of use; 6= advertisement; 7= alteration & advertisement; 9= no entry).

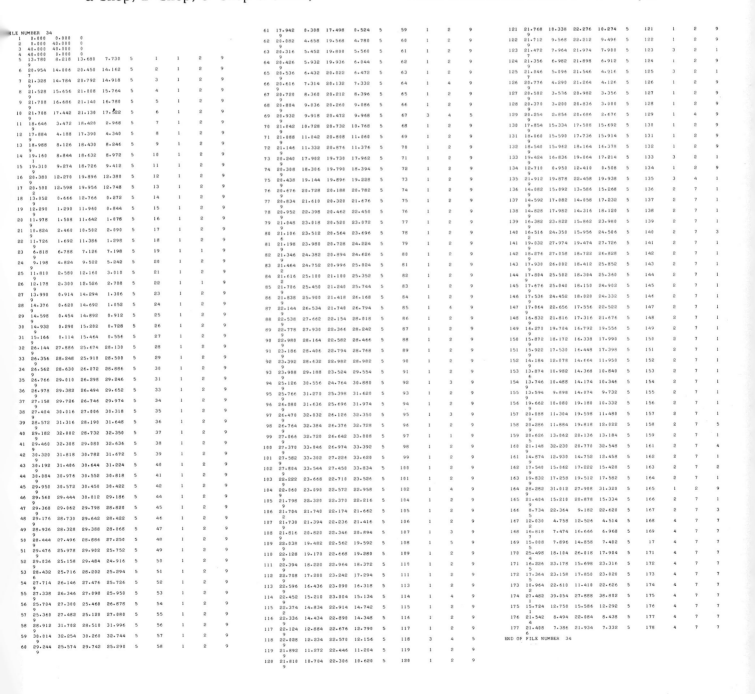

ILE NUMBER 34

I	II	III	IV	V	VI	VII	VIII	IX	X	XI
1	0.000	0.000	0							
2	0.000	40.000	0							
3	40.000	40.000	0							
4	40.000	0.000	0							
5	13.780	8.218	13.680	7.730	5	1	1	2	9	9
6	20.954	14.006	20.450	14.162	5	2	1	2	9	7
7	21.328	14.784	20.792	14.918	5	3	1	2	9	9
8	21.528	15.656	21.008	15.764	5	4	1	2	9	9
9	21.708	16.686	21.140	16.780	5	5	1	2	9	9
10	21.708	17.442	21.130	17.522	5	6	1	2	9	9
11	18.646	3.472	18.420	2.968	5	7	1	2	9	9
12	17.884	4.188	17.390	4.340	5	8	1	2	9	9
13	18.988	8.126	18.430	8.246	5	9	1	2	9	9
14	19.160	8.844	18.632	8.972	5	10	1	2	9	1
15	19.310	9.274	18.726	9.412	5	11	1	2	9	9
16	20.380	12.270	19.896	12.380	5	12	1	2	9	9
17	20.500	12.598	19.956	12.748	5	13	1	2	9	2
18	13.052	0.666	12.766	0.272	5	14	1	2	9	9
19	12.290	1.290	11.960	0.844	5	15	1	2	9	9
20	11.978	1.508	11.642	1.078	5	16	1	2	9	9
21	10.824	2.460	10.502	2.090	5	17	1	2	9	9
22	11.726	1.692	11.386	1.298	5	18	1	2	9	9
23	6.818	6.788	7.126	7.198	5	19	1	1	9	9
24	9.198	4.824	9.522	5.242	5	20	1	2	9	9
25	11.810	2.580	12.160	3.010	5	21	1	2	9	9
26	12.178	2.300	12.526	2.708	5	22	1	1	9	9
27	13.990	0.914	14.294	1.306	5	23	1	2	9	9
28	14.376	0.620	14.692	1.052	5	24	1	2	9	9
29	14.598	0.454	14.892	0.912	5	25	1	2	9	9
30	14.932	0.290	15.202	0.728	5	26	1	2	9	9
31	15.166	0.114	15.464	0.556	5	27	1	2	9	9
32	26.144	27.886	25.674	28.130	5	28	1	2	9	9
33	26.356	28.248	25.910	28.500	5	29	1	2	9	9
34	26.562	28.630	26.072	28.886	5	30	1	2	9	9
35	26.766	29.010	26.298	29.246	5	31	1	2	9	9
36	26.978	29.382	26.494	29.652	5	33	1	2	9	9
37	27.158	29.726	26.746	29.974	5	34	1	2	9	9
38	27.404	30.016	27.006	30.318	5	35	1	2	9	9
39	28.572	31.316	28.190	31.648	5	36	1	2	9	9
40	29.182	32.002	28.732	32.350	5	37	1	2	9	9
41	29.460	32.308	29.080	32.636	5	38	1	2	9	9
42	30.320	31.818	30.782	31.672	5	39	1	2	9	9
43	30.192	31.406	30.644	31.224	5	40	1	2	9	9
44	30.084	30.976	30.552	30.818	5	41	1	2	9	9
45	29.950	30.572	30.450	30.422	5	42	1	2	9	9
46	29.560	29.444	30.012	29.186	5	44	1	2	9	9
47	29.368	29.062	29.798	28.820	5	45	1	2	9	9
48	29.176	28.730	29.642	28.422	5	46	1	2	9	9
49	28.936	28.328	29.388	28.068	5	47	1	2	9	9
50	28.444	27.496	28.886	27.250	5	48	1	2	9	9
51	29.476	25.978	29.902	25.752	5	49	1	2	9	9
52	29.036	25.158	29.484	24.916	5	50	1	2	9	9
53	28.432	25.716	28.202	25.294	5	51	1	2	9	6
54	27.714	26.146	27.476	25.726	5	52	1	2	9	9
55	27.338	26.346	27.098	25.950	5	53	1	2	9	9
56	25.704	27.300	25.460	26.878	5	54	1	2	9	9
57	25.360	27.482	25.120	27.080	5	55	1	2	9	9
58	28.912	31.702	28.510	31.996	5	56	1	2	9	9
59	30.014	32.254	30.260	32.744	5	57	1	2	9	9
60	29.244	25.574	29.742	25.290	5	58	1	2	9	9
61	17.942	0.308	17.498	0.524	5	59	1	2	9	9
62	20.082	4.658	19.568	4.780	5	60	1	2	9	9
63	20.316	5.452	19.800	5.560	5	61	1	2	9	9
64	20.426	5.932	19.936	6.044	5	62	1	2	9	9
65	20.536	6.432	20.022	6.472	5	63	1	2	9	9
66	20.616	7.314	20.132	7.332	5	64	1	4	9	9
67	20.720	8.360	20.212	8.396	5	65	1	2	9	9
68	20.804	9.036	20.260	9.086	5	66	1	2	9	9
69	20.932	9.918	20.472	9.968	5	67	3	4	5	9
70	21.042	10.728	20.732	10.768	5	68	1	2	9	9
71	21.088	11.042	20.808	11.060	5	69	1	2	9	9
72	21.146	11.332	20.876	11.376	5	70	1	2	9	9
73	20.240	17.902	19.730	17.962	5	71	1	2	9	9
74	20.308	18.306	19.790	18.394	5	72	1	2	9	9
75	20.438	19.144	19.896	19.228	5	73	1	2	9	9
76	20.676	20.728	20.188	20.782	5	74	1	2	9	9
77	20.834	21.610	20.320	21.676	5	75	1	2	9	9
78	20.952	22.398	20.462	22.450	5	76	1	2	9	9
79	21.048	23.018	20.520	23.072	5	77	1	2	9	9
80	21.106	23.512	20.564	23.696	5	78	1	2	9	6
81	21.198	23.980	20.728	24.224	5	79	1	2	9	9
82	21.346	24.382	20.894	24.626	5	80	1	2	9	9
83	21.464	24.752	20.996	25.024	5	81	1	2	9	2
84	21.616	25.100	21.100	25.352	5	82	1	2	9	2
85	21.706	25.450	21.240	25.744	5	83	1	2	9	9
86	21.838	25.900	21.418	26.168	5	84	1	2	9	9
87	22.144	26.534	21.740	26.794	5	85	1	6	9	9
88	22.538	27.662	22.154	28.018	5	86	1	2	9	9
89	22.778	27.930	22.366	28.242	5	87	1	2	9	9
90	22.980	28.164	22.582	28.466	5	88	1	2	9	9
91	23.186	28.406	22.794	28.768	5	89	1	2	9	9
92	23.392	28.632	22.982	28.982	5	90	1	2	9	9
93	23.908	29.188	23.524	29.554	5	91	1	2	9	9
94	25.126	30.556	24.764	30.880	5	92	1	3	9	9
95	25.766	31.270	25.398	31.620	5	93	1	2	9	9
96	26.080	31.636	25.696	31.974	5	94	1	2	9	9
97	26.470	32.032	26.126	32.350	5	95	1	3	9	9
98	26.764	32.384	26.376	32.728	5	96	1	2	9	9
99	27.066	32.720	26.642	33.008	5	97	1	1	9	9
100	27.370	33.046	26.974	33.392	5	98	1	2	9	9
101	27.582	33.302	27.226	33.620	5	99	1	2	9	9
102	27.804	33.544	27.450	33.834	5	100	1	2	9	9
103	22.222	23.668	22.710	23.526	5	101	1	2	9	9
104	22.060	23.090	22.572	22.958	5	102	1	4	9	9
105	21.798	22.320	22.370	22.216	5	104	1	2	9	9
106	21.704	21.740	22.174	21.662	5	105	1	2	9	2
107	21.730	21.394	22.236	21.416	5	106	1	2	9	9
108	21.816	20.820	22.346	20.894	5	107	1	3	9	9
109	22.038	19.482	22.562	19.592	5	108	1	5	9	9
110	22.128	19.170	22.668	19.280	5	109	1	2	9	9
111	22.394	18.220	22.964	18.372	5	110	1	2	9	9
112	22.708	17.200	23.242	17.294	5	111	1	2	9	9
113	22.596	16.436	23.090	16.318	5	113	1	2	9	9
114	22.452	15.210	23.004	15.134	5	114	1	4	9	9
115	22.374	14.834	22.914	14.742	5	115	1	2	9	2
116	22.336	14.434	22.890	14.348	5	116	1	2	9	9
117	22.124	12.884	22.676	12.790	5	117	1	2	9	9
118	22.028	12.234	22.570	12.156	5	118	3	4	5	9
119	21.892	11.272	22.446	11.204	5	119	1	2	9	9
120	21.810	10.704	22.306	10.620	5	120	1	2	9	9
121	21.768	10.338	22.276	10.274	5	121	1	2	9	9
122	21.712	9.568	22.212	9.496	5	122	1	2	9	9
123	21.472	7.964	21.974	7.900	5	123	3	2	1	7
124	21.356	6.982	21.898	6.912	5	124	1	2	9	9
125	21.046	5.096	21.546	4.916	5	125	3	2	1	7
126	20.776	4.290	21.264	4.126	5	126	1	2	9	9
127	20.502	3.536	20.982	3.356	5	127	1	2	9	9
128	20.370	3.200	20.836	3.000	5	128	1	2	9	9
129	20.254	2.856	20.686	2.676	5	129	1	4	9	9
130	17.854	15.334	17.508	15.692	5	130	1	2	9	9
131	18.060	15.590	17.736	15.914	5	131	1	2	9	9
132	18.540	15.962	18.164	16.378	5	132	1	2	9	9
133	19.424	16.836	19.064	17.214	5	133	3	2	1	9
134	12.710	0.950	12.410	0.508	5	134	1	2	9	9
135	21.912	19.878	22.458	19.938	5	135	3	4	1	9
136	14.082	15.092	13.586	15.268	5	136	2	7	1	9
137	14.592	17.082	14.058	17.232	5	137	2	7	1	9
138	14.828	17.982	14.316	18.120	5	138	2	7	1	9
139	16.382	23.822	15.862	23.980	5	139	2	7	1	9
140	16.516	24.350	15.956	24.506	5	140	2	7	3	2
141	19.032	27.974	19.474	27.726	5	141	2	7	1	9
142	18.276	27.058	18.722	26.828	5	142	2	7	1	9
143	17.930	26.002	18.412	25.852	5	143	2	7	1	9
144	17.804	25.502	18.304	25.360	5	144	2	7	1	9
145	17.676	25.040	18.150	24.902	5	145	2	7	1	9
146	17.536	24.452	18.020	24.332	5	146	2	7	1	9
147	17.064	22.656	17.556	22.522	5	147	2	7	1	9
148	16.832	21.816	17.316	21.676	5	148	2	7	1	9
149	16.270	19.704	16.792	19.556	5	149	2	7	1	9
150	15.872	18.172	16.338	17.990	5	150	2	7	1	9
151	15.922	17.530	16.448	17.398	5	151	2	7	1	9
152	14.184	12.078	14.664	11.950	5	152	2	7	1	9
153	13.874	10.982	14.368	10.840	5	153	2	7	1	6
154	13.746	10.488	14.174	10.346	5	154	2	7	1	9
155	13.594	9.898	14.074	9.732	5	155	2	7	1	9
156	19.662	10.080	19.180	10.332	5	156	2	7	1	9
157	20.088	11.304	19.598	11.480	5	157	2	7	1	9
158	20.286	11.884	19.818	12.022	5	158	2	7	5	9
159	20.626	13.062	20.136	13.184	5	159	2	7	1	5
160	21.148	32.230	20.770	32.548	5	161	2	7	4	9
161	14.874	12.930	14.752	12.458	5	162	2	7	1	9
162	17.540	15.062	17.222	15.428	5	163	2	7	2	9
163	19.832	17.258	19.512	17.582	5	164	2	7	1	9
164	28.282	31.012	27.908	31.320	5	165	1	2	9	9
165	21.404	15.210	20.878	15.334	5	166	2	7	1	9
166	8.734	22.364	9.182	22.620	5	167	2	7	3	5
167	12.030	4.758	12.526	4.514	5	168	4	7	7	2
168	16.818	7.474	16.666	6.968	5	169	4	7	7	7
169	15.008	7.896	14.858	7.402	5	17	4	7	7	5
170	25.498	18.104	26.018	17.904	5	171	4	7	7	4
171	16.226	23.178	15.698	23.316	5	172	4	7	7	5
172	17.364	23.158	17.850	23.020	5	173	4	7	7	5
173	10.964	22.610	11.410	22.626	5	174	4	7	7	2
174	27.482	39.054	27.888	38.802	5	175	4	7	7	1
175	15.724	12.750	15.586	12.292	5	176	4	7	7	1
176	21.542	8.494	22.084	8.438	5	177	4	7	7	4
177	21.408	7.386	21.934	7.332	5	178	4	7	7	6

END OF FILE NUMBER 34

LAMBETH
Streatham High Road

Commercial premises - from
the rating file

▮	Shop & house
▯	Shop & cafe
│	Office
▐	Ground & undefined floor
▬	Second floor
○	Other & multiple floors

Scale 1:1250

Commercial premises-
planning permissions-from
the CLUSTER file

New shop
New office
Office to shop
Additional use
Intra-category change

Scale 1:1250

COVENTRY
Eagle Street Action Area–part

Existing land use – from a
planning map

Scale 1:1250

4

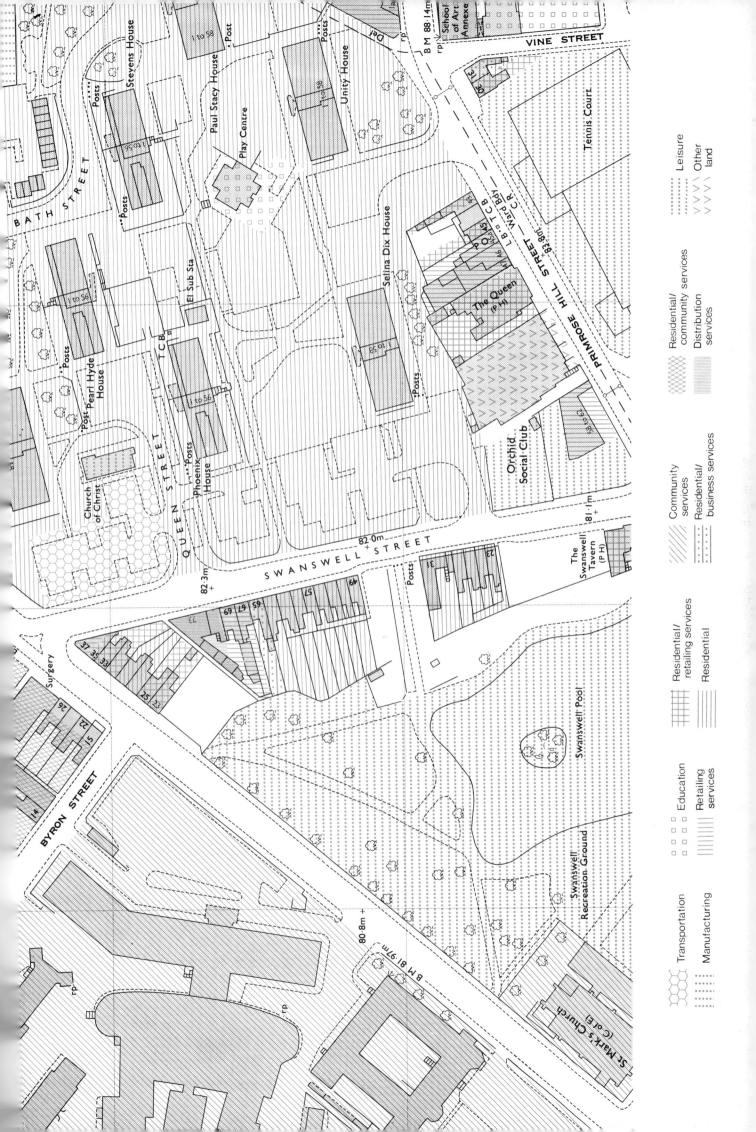

VINE STREET

School of Art Annexe
BM 88·14m

Stevens House
Posts
1 to 58
Post
Posts

Unity House
58

BATH STREET

Paul Stacy House
Play Centre

Tennis Court

PRIMROSE HILL STREET

1 to 56

El Sub Sta

Selina Dix House

P.O. 45 TCB
LB 46 Ward Bdy
CR
83·8m

The Queen
(PH)

Posts
Post Pearl Hyde House
TCB
QUEEN STREET
1 to 56
Posts
Phoenix House
Posts

85 to 1
Posts

Church of Christ

82·3m

82·0m
SWANSWELL STREET

Orchid Social Club

69 to 58

69 67
65
57
73
49
31
23

Surgery
26
22
15
14

37 35 33
25 23

BYRON STREET

The Swanswell Tavern (PH)
81·1m

Swanswell Pool

Swanswell Recreation Ground

80·8m

BM 81·97m

St Mark's Church (C of E)

Transportation

Manufacturing

Community services

Education

Retailing services

Residential/retailing services

Residential

Residential/community services

Distribution services

Residential/business services

Leisure

Other land

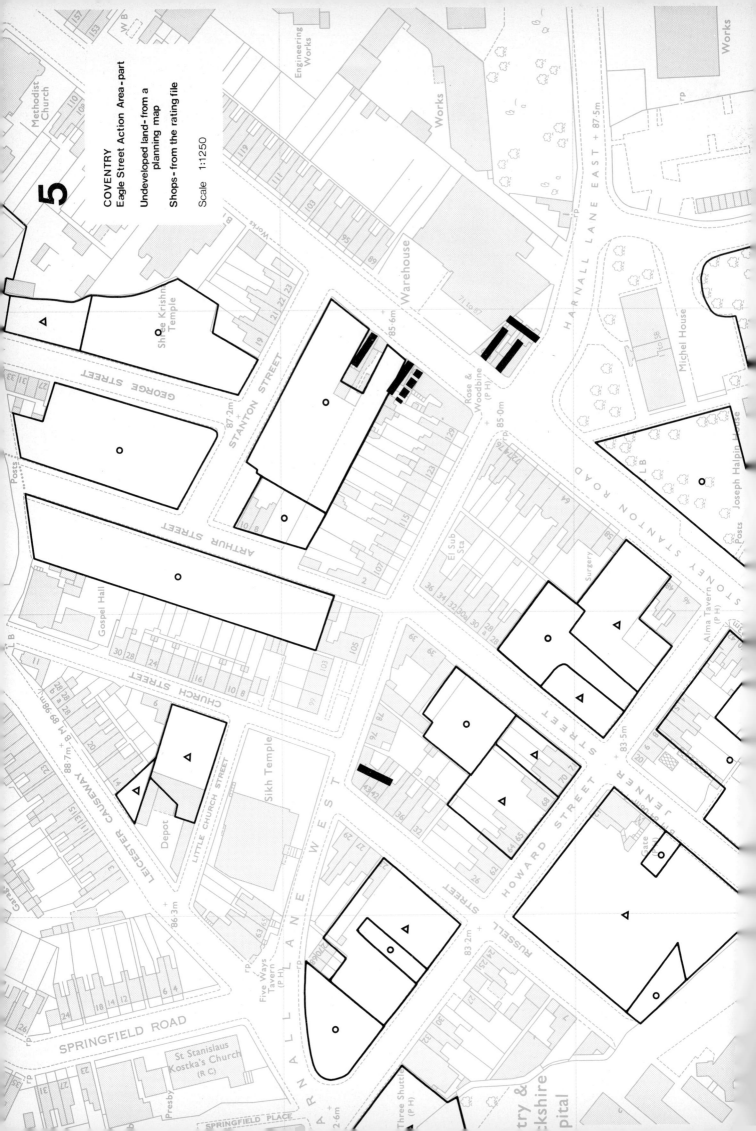

5

COVENTRY
Eagle Street Action Area - part

Undeveloped land - from a
planning map

Shops - from the rating file

Scale 1:1250

Methodist
Church

Engineering
Works

Works

Works

HARNALL LANE EAST + 87.5m

Shree Krishna
Temple

GEORGE STREET

STANTON STREET

Warehouse

71 to 87

Rose &
Woodbine
(P H)

85.0m

Michel House

Joseph Halpin House

ARTHUR STREET

El Sub
Sta

Surgery

STONEY STANTON ROAD

LB

Gospel Hall

CHURCH STREET

LEICESTER CAUSEWAY

88.7m

86.3m

Depot

LITTLE CHURCH STREET

Sikh Temple

HOWARD STREET

RUSSELL STREET

83.5m

JENNER STREET

Alma Tavern
(P H)

83.2m

SPRINGFIELD ROAD

St Stanislaus
Kostka's Church
(R C)

Presby

Five Ways
Tavern (P H)

HARNALL LANE WEST

Three Shuttles
(P H)

82.6m

SPRINGFIELD PLACE

Coventry &
Warwickshire
Hospital

VINE STREET

BATH STREET

Stevens House

Paul Stacy House

Play Centre

Unity House

El Sub Sta

Pearl Hyde House

Selina Dix House

Phoenix House

QUEEN STREET

Church of Christ

The Queen (P.H)

PRIMROSE HILL STREET

83.8m

Ward Bdy

CR

CB

Tennis Court

82.0m

82.3m

SWANSWELL STREET

Orchid Social Club

The Swanswell Tavern (P.H)

Post

Surgery

BYRON STREET

Swanswell Pool

Swanswell Recreation Ground

80.8m

BM 81.97m

St Mark's Church (C of E)

Shops

▬▬▬ Shop

▪▪▪▪ Shop & house/flat or house & workshop

▮▮▮▮ House/flat shop & garage

▥▥▥ Shop & office

Undeveloped land

△ Council ownership

○ Private ownership

6

HAMPSHIRE
Central Winchester

Time period 1975

Commercial premises – from
the rating file

▲ Offices

▲ All shops

◄ Other commercial premises
— Public house
······ Restaurant
·-· Hotel

Change of owner ►
Change of owner 1971-75

Non-resident ratepayers ▶

Vacant premises ▶

Outstanding planning permissions
— New premise
┊ Extension
┈▶ Change of use

Commercial premises-from planning files

Completed planning permissions
— Extension
┈▶ Change of use

◻ Car Park

Input scale 1:1250
Output scale 1:10,560

Study area ▶

Study area ▶

Study area ▶

Study area ▶

WINCHESTER

Study area ▶

HAMPSHIRE
Central Winchester

Commercial premises-from
the rating file

Rateable value in £'s

Ground & undefined	← Floor level →	Above ground

0 - 499

500 - 999

1000 - 2499

2500 - 4999

5000 - 9999

10 000 & over

Scale   1:2500

Public Library

Car Park

Odeon Theatre

Tanks

Car Park

P C

T C Bs

Shelter

L B

St Peter's R C Church

BM 42·69m

Cambria House

Presbytery

Convent

Milner Hall

Methodist Church

El Sub Sta

Hall

Well

42·1m

BM 46·6m

JEWRY STREET

ST PETER STREET

PARCHMENT STREET

Hall

BM 46·85m

Hall

BM 43·58m

United Reformed Church

rp

Jewry Garages

Methodist Church

Royal Hotel

41·8m

Telephone Exchange

T C B

The Fountain Head (P H)

41·1m

Bank

ST GEORGE'S STREET

The Royal Oak (P H)

God Begot House

Posts

Hall

Bank

Ward Bdy

C R

HIGH STREET

104

106

107

Pond

Posts

St George

Bank

P H

Bank

Bank

106

107

102

108

110

111

Parchment St

ST GEORGE

36·9m

LB

Cross

Posts

3·81m + The Pentice

BM 37·34m

ST CLEMENT STREET

Church (C of E)

118 to 121

Upper Brook Street

HIGH

El Sub Sta

Car Park

P H

Old Market House

Bank

ST THOMAS STREET

THE

8

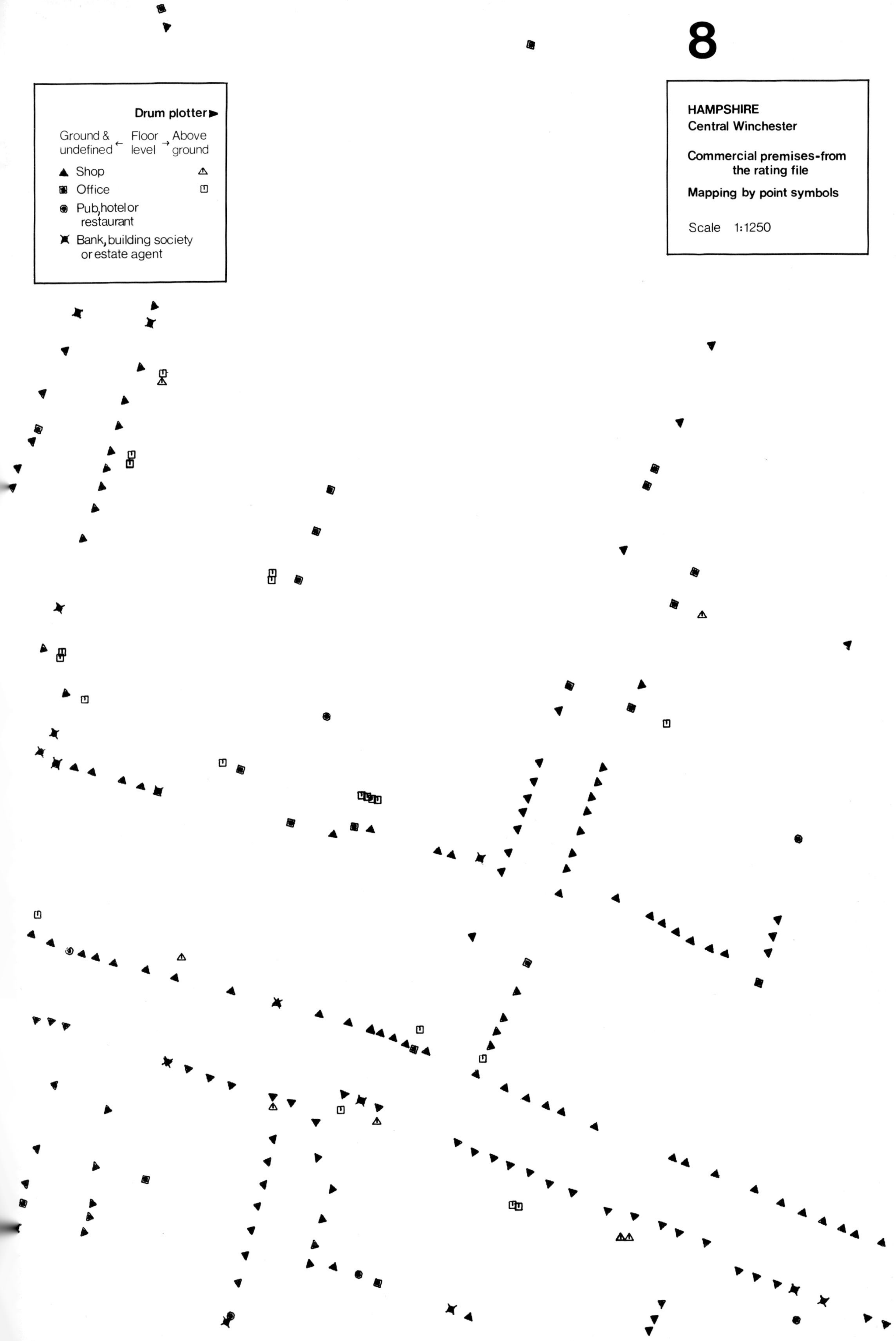

HAMPSHIRE
Central Winchester

Commercial premises-from
the rating file

Mapping by point symbols

Scale   1:1250

Drum plotter▶

Ground &   Floor   → Above
undefined ← level → ground

▲ Shop   △

▨ Office   ▯

◉ Pub, hotel or
   restaurant

✕ Bank, building society
   or estate agent

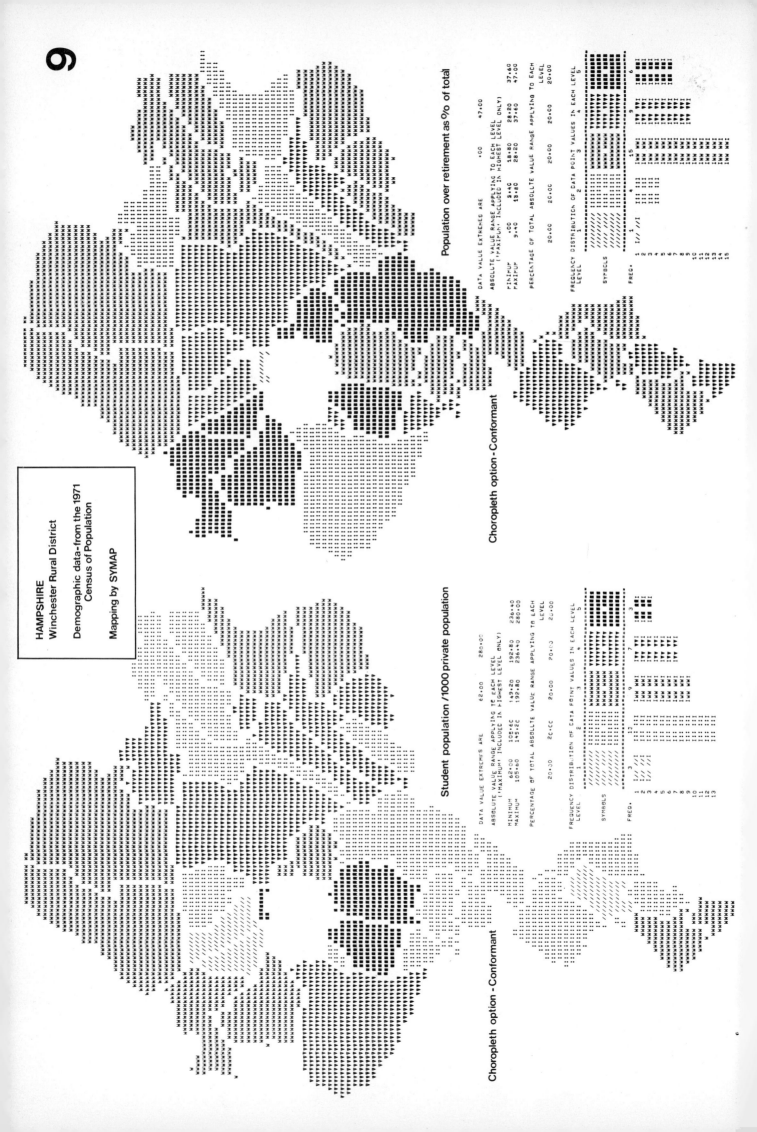

9

HAMPSHIRE
Winchester Rural District

Demographic data-from the 1971
Census of Population

Mapping by SYMAP

Population over retirement as % of total

Choropleth option - Conformant

Student population /1000 private population

Choropleth option - Conformant

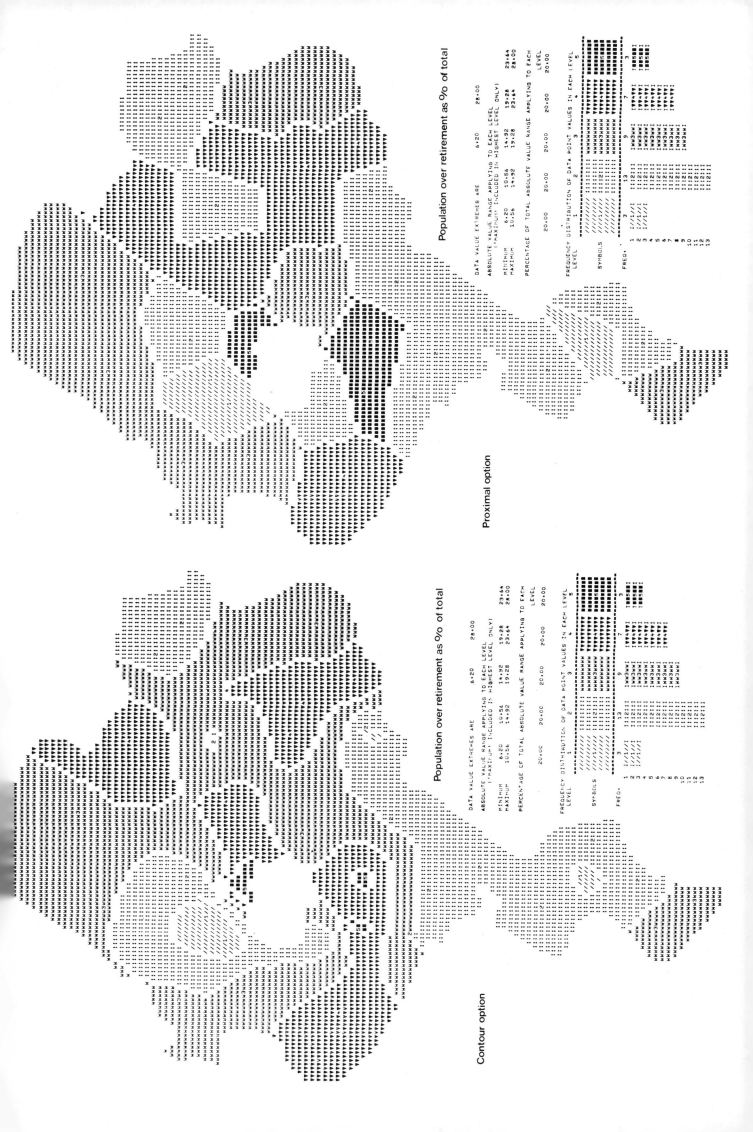

Population over retirement as % of total

Proximal option

Population over retirement as % of total

Contour option

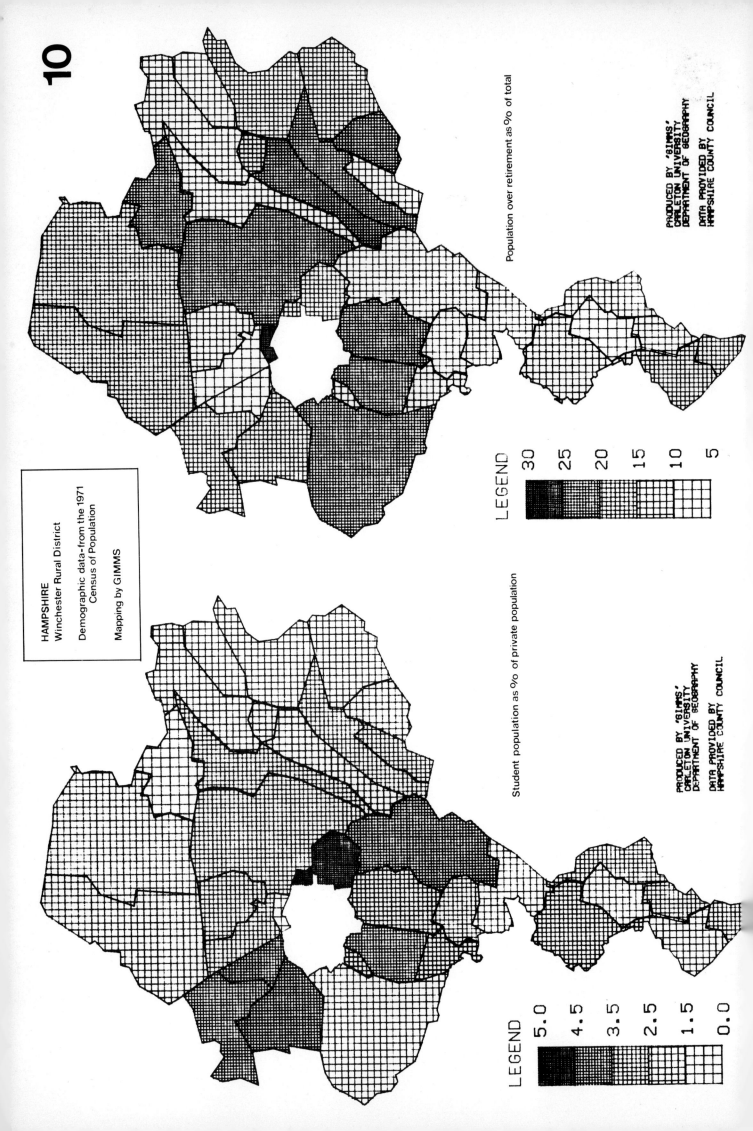

10

HAMPSHIRE
Winchester Rural District

Demographic data - from the 1971
Census of Population

Mapping by GIMMS

Population over retirement as % of total

LEGEND
30
25
20
15
10
5

Student population as % of private population

LEGEND
5.0
4.5
3.5
2.5
1.5
0.0

PRODUCED BY 'GIMMS'
CARLETON UNIVERSITY
DEPARTMENT OF GEOGRAPHY

DATA PROVIDED BY
HAMPSHIRE COUNTY COUNCIL

PRODUCED BY 'GIMMS'
CARLETON UNIVERSITY
DEPARTMENT OF GEOGRAPHY

DATA PROVIDED BY
HAMPSHIRE COUNTY COUNCIL

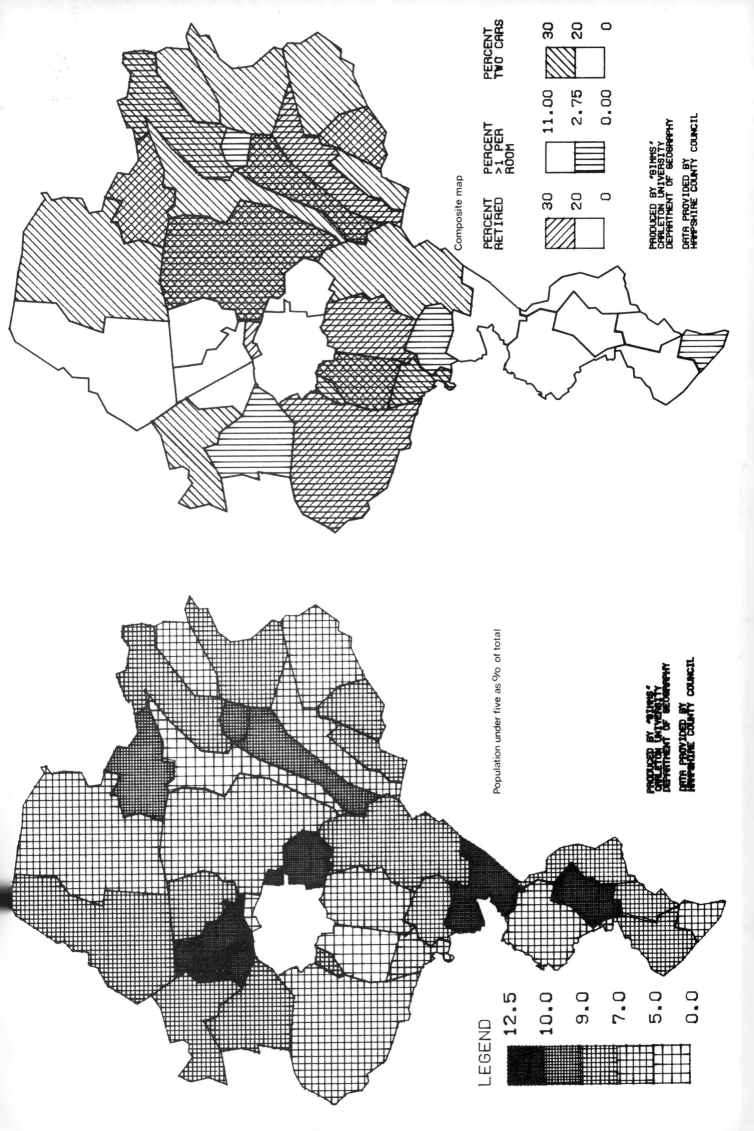

Composite map

PERCENT
RETIRED

30

20

0

PERCENT
>1 PER
ROOM

11.00

2.75

0.00

PERCENT
TWO CARS

30

20

0

PRODUCED BY 'BIMMS'
CARLETON UNIVERSITY
DEPARTMENT OF GEOGRAPHY

DATA PROVIDED BY
HAMPSHIRE COUNTY COUNCIL

Population under five as % of total

LEGEND

12.5

10.0

9.0

7.0

5.0

0.0

PRODUCED BY 'BIMMS'
CARLETON UNIVERSITY
DEPARTMENT OF GEOGRAPHY

DATA PROVIDED BY
HAMPSHIRE COUNTY COUNCIL

Demographic data - from the 1971
Census of Population

Total population
1mm : 200 persons

Females 60 & over
Males 65 & over
Children 0 - 4
Children 5 - 14
1mm : 1%

Each parish has one
symbol

Scale 1:100 000

11

NORFOLK
South Norfolk-part

Bus services - from a
planning file

Cars - from the Census of
Population 1971

Shops - from the rating file

Population change -
from the Census
of Population 1971

Car owners as % of total
population. 1mm: 5%

Number of shops
1mm: 1shop

Population change as %
1961-71
Increase
Decrease } 1mm: 2%

Each parish has one
symbol

Frequency of bus services
⊥⊥⊥ 1 weekday
╫╫╫ 1 weekday & saturday
╫╫ 2,3 or 4 days monday-friday
——— Daily monday-saturday

Scale 1:100 000

12

NEWCASTLE UPON TYNE
Central City

Office floorspace - from the 1974
          planning office land use file

Mapping by Linmap

Percentage of total floorspace by street block

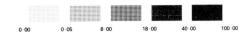

0·00   0·05   8·00   18·00   40·00   100·00

SCALE   1:15000   (0.24 MILES TO 1 INCH)

VALUATION LIST DESCRIPTIONS FOR LAND USE

Numbers and rateable values of hereditaments (Supplied by DOE as of 1/4/75 for England and Wales

		CV/R/140 Code	Rateable Values £M	Hereditaments (000s)	% to which NLUC codes allocated
1.	Total Domestic	1999	£3261	17204 (83%)	100%
	of which houses, maisonettes, flats, etc. (other than agricultural dwelling houses).	1099	£3188	16838	100%
2.	Total Commercial	2999	£1686	2984 (14.4%)	85%
	of which lock-up garages (separately assessed);	2100	£ 28	1734	100%
	shops (incl. banks in shopping areas) and cafes.	2020	£ 501	398	79%
3.	Total Industrial Undertakings	3999	£ 810	105 (0.5%)	86%
	of which factories, mills and other premises of a similar character.	3010	£ 792	101	89%
4.	Total Other Undertakings	4999	£ 334	39 (0.2%)	98%
	of which Electricity	4020	£ 160	1	100%
	Post Office	4050	£ 64	20	100%
5.	Total Entertainment and Recreation	5999	£ 69	71 (0.3%)	92%
	of which social clubs, community centres & public halls.	5040	£ 29	47	100%
6.	Total Education and Culture	6999	£ 216	42 (0.2%)	65%
	of which schools and colleges (Local Authority)	6020	£ 166	31	79%
7.	Total Miscellaneous	7999	£ 366	283 (1.4%)	80%
	Total	9999	£6742	20728	97%

VALUATION LIST DESCRIPTIONS FOR LAND USE

(a)   The purpose of this appendix is to assess the classification problems that would arise in handling land use information derived from the Valuations Lists if the proposed system of coded property descriptions were introduced by the Valuation Office. Two points have, of course, been made in the main report: first, that these lists quantify (in value terms) what they describe; and second, that they locate in terms of postal address and not by geocode. The classification problems would be rather more complex in detail, and no direct, one-for-one, relationship with the National Land Use Classification (NLUC) would exist. It must be emphasised that the concern here is to translate <u>from</u> the proposed Valuation List descriptions <u>to</u> land use classes: in the present context the translation would only need to be one-way.

(b)   The general setting of the problem is indicated by the table for England and Wales on the facing page, which uses the seven prime "categories" found in Valuation Lists, and certain of the subdivisions of these into the (49) "classifications" that are used in the statistical analysis forms CV/R/140, as reproduced on the next pages. The right hand column of this table shows the percentage of hereditaments for which it appears that equivalent NLUC codes could be given. The high degree of compatibility is encouraging.

(c)   Valuation descriptions of property given by Valuation Officers are, of course, far more detailed than those shown in the CV/R/140 forms (which represent a generalised grouping of classes requested by the Department of the Environment). At present these detailed descriptions do not have any overall numerical coding system; however, the Inland Revenue have been considering the introduction of codes as part of a possible move to computerise the large amount of data involved. Although these codes are still under discussion, the examples of the primary code descriptions in Table 1 (from the Inland Revenue) are based on descriptions appearing in the 1973 computer-printed Valuation Lists.

(d)   The system of codes being considered for these purposes assumes a primary code (5 digits) plus a secondary code (4 digits). It seems worth studying the organisation of these codes. The proposed initial 5-digit primary code is based on a hierarchy of four levels, and some examples are given in Table 1.

County...

Rating
Area ....

*L.B.
Dist:

L.A. Code ☐☐☐☐☐☐☐☐

*Strike out
whichever is inapplicable

STATISTICAL ANALYSIS OF NUMBERS AND RATEABLE VALUES
OF ALL HEREDITAMENTS SHOWN IN THE VALUATION LIST
ON..

Classification	Code	Numbers	R.V.	Extended Totals for each Category	
				Numbers	R.V.
DOMESTIC	1.		£		£
Houses, Maisonettes, Flats, Caravans, etc. (other than Agricultural Dwelling Houses) with Rateable Values:–					
Not exceeding £75	1010				
Exceeding £75 but not exceeding £100 ...	1020				
„ £100 „ £125 ...	1030				
„ £125 „ £150 ...	1040				
„ £150 „ £400 ...	1050				
„ £400	1060				
TOTALS	1099				
Agricultural Dwelling Houses (of all Rateable Values)	1110				
Crown Dwelling Houses	1120				
Separately assessed Single Caravan Sites ...	1210				
TOTALS FOR CATEGORY 1	1999				
COMMERCIAL	2.				
Shops assessed with Private Dwelling Accommodation	2010				
Shops (including Banks in Shopping Areas) and Cafes	2020				
Offices (including Banks in Office Areas) ...	2030				
Public Houses including Beerhouses	2040				
Hotels and Boarding Houses	2050				
Restaurants	2060				
Holiday Camps and Caravan Fields	2070				
Warehouses, Stores and Workshops	2080				
Garages (commercial), Petrol Filling Stations and Car Parks	2090				
Lock up Garages (separately assessed) ...	2100				
Advertising Stations and Rights	2110				
Markets	2120				
TOTALS FOR CATEGORY 2	2999				
INDUSTRIAL UNDERTAKINGS	3.				
Factories, Mills and other premises of a similar character	3010				
Mineral Producing Hereditaments (other than National Coal Board hereditaments assessed under S.35 2(a) G.R. Act 1967)	3020				
TOTALS FOR CATEGORY 3	3999				
			Carried forward ...		

Classification	Code	Numbers	R.V.	Extended Totals for each Category	
				Numbers	R.V.
			£		£
OTHER UNDERTAKINGS	4.	Brought	forward	....	....
Gas	4010				
Electricity	4020				
National Coal Board (heridataments referred to in S.35 2(a) G.R. Act 1967)...	4030				
Water	4040				
Post Office ... .:	4050				
Docks, Harbours, Canals, etc.	4060				
Other Transport (including Ferries, Toll Bridges, Road Transport Depots and Yards, etc.) ...	4070				
TOTALS FOR CATEGORY 4	4999				
ENTERTAINMENT AND RECREATIONAL	5.				
Cinemas	5010				
Theatres and Music Halls	5020				
Sports and Recreational Grounds, Golf Courses and Race Courses	5030				
Social Clubs, Community Centres and Public Halls	5040				
Residential Clubs	5050				
Other Places of Entertainment or Recreation (such as Billiards Saloons, Bowling Alleys, Dance Halls, Pleasure Parks, Foreshores, Swimming Pools, Fairgrounds and the like) ...	5060				
Radio, Television and Relay Undertakings ...	5070				
TOTALS FOR CATEGORY 5	5999				
EDUCATIONAL AND CULTURAL	6.				
Libraries, Museums, Art Galleries, etc. ...	6010				
Schools and Colleges (Local Authority) ...	6020				
Schools and Colleges (Non Local Authority)...	6030				
Universities and University Colleges	6040				
TOTALS FOR CATEGORY 6	6999				
MISCELLANEOUS	7.				
Crown occupations (including National Health Hospitals, Clinics, etc. but excluding Dwellings)	7010				
Other Hospitals, Clinics, Nursing Homes, etc.	7020				
Public Wash-Houses and Baths	7030				
Cemeteries, Crematoria and Columbaria ...	7040				
Sewage Disposal Works and Refuse Disposal Works	7050				
Town Halls and Municipal Offices	7060				
Hereditaments not otherwise classified ...	7070				
TOTALS FOR CATEGORY 7	7999			....	....
TOTALS FOR ALL CATEGORIES IN THE VALUATION LIST 9999					

I certify that the information in this form is correct.

....Valuation Officer ....197........

....Valuation Area

                                        844/4 Dd083224 600pads 1/76 RG.Ltd. 468

(e)   The proposed first level of <u>category</u> (1-digit) signifies whether the property is one of the following:

Category	Code number
Domestic	1
Commercial	2
Industrial Undertakings	3
Other Undertakings	4
Entertainment and Recreation	5
Education and Culture	6
Miscellaneous	7
Non-rated (Land	8
(Spare	9 & 0

These are also the major headings of Statistical Analysis of Rated Hereditaments (CV/R/140) with the addition of non-rated land and spare categories, codes 8, 9 and 0.

(f)   The proposed second level or <u>classification</u> (1-digit) signifies the particular sub-classes of each of the first level categories. For example, the sub-classes of "Commercial" are:

Classification	Code number
Shops assessed with Private Dwelling Accommodation.	1
Shops (including Banks in Shopping Areas, Cafes and Restaurants.	2
Offices (including Banks in Office Areas)	3
Public Houses (including Beer Houses), Hotels Boarding Houses and Restaurants.	4
Holiday Camps and Caravan Camps	5
Warehouses, Stores and Workshops	6
Garages (commercial), Petrol Filling Stations and Car Parks.	7
Lock-up Garages (separately assessed)	8
Advertising Stations and Rights	9
Markets	0

(g)   The proposed third level or <u>group</u> (1-digit) again signifies particular subdivisions of the second level. For example, the subdivisions of "Offices" are:

Group	Code number
Offices	1
Banks in Office Area	2
Centres	3
Specific Offices	4
Surgeries and Consulting Rooms	5

(h)   The proposed fourth level or <u>class</u> (2 digits) yet again signifies subdivisions of the third level. For example, the subdivisions of "Specific Offices" are:

Class	Code number
Betting Office	01
Booking Office	02
Employment Exchange	03
Estate Office	04
Inspector's Office	05
Ticket Office	06
Transport Office	07

(j)   The full Primary code of an estate office therefore would be 23404

comprising 2 = Commercial.............Category level
3 = Offices (including.........Classification level
Banks in Office Areas)
4 = Specific office............Group level
04 = Estate Office.............Class level

(k)   In addition to this Primary code a set of Secondary 4-digit codes are also proposed. These mainly cope with ancillary uses, e.g. shop and garage. Table 2 shows two pages selected at random from the full list of Secondary codes (which is a 27-page document). To extend the example above, the Secondary code would describe an estate office and car park by adding 0200. Thus the full composite code for such a property would be 234040200. It should be noted that, if adopted, Valuation List descriptions are all planned to have full 9-digit codes, and in the many cases where a Secondary code is unnecessary "filling" may be employed, i.e. the addition of zeros.

(l)   Table 1, which shows some examples of the proposed primary descriptions, also shows what we suggest are the nearest equivalent NLUC codes (right hand column): these are alphanumeric. The example of Estate Office used above translates into OFOIA-E in the codings of NLUC.

As in most translation, there are discrepancies in detail. There is, for example, no precise equivalent for "delicensed beer house". To code it as "beer house" would be manifestly inaccurate. For obvious reasons, no attempt has been made to translate the secondary codes of the Valuations Lists to NLUC terms.

(m)   The main conclusion of the study is to point to the large measure of direct translation into NLUC terms that it seems would be possible for the vast majority of hereditaments. A minority of curiosities and untranslatables are inevitable in any two classification systems set up separately and for different purposes. If the system of coded descriptions is adopted by the Inland Revenue Valuation Office, it will then be for local authority planners to decide whether these discrepancies debar the use of Valuation List data as a source of land use.

(n)   If the Valuation List were to be computerised on a national basis, the extraction of data relating to land use would undoubtedly be improved. However, should this not be the case, information may still be extracted from existing records, manual or computerised depending upon the local authority, as evidenced by the maps in Appendix I. The absence of an overall computerised system would not invalidate the use of this source of data.

TABLE 1

Proposed Primary Descriptions of the Valuation List -
some examples from the draft hierarchical list of codes.

Annotated with codes of the National Land Use Classification.

These codes are at present undergoing revision.

Primary description hierarchy from the
Inland Revenue Valuation Office (1975)

National Land Classification (DOE 1975)

Annotations suggested by ECU (1976)

Not over £75	£75-£100	£101-£125	£126-£150	£151-£400	Over £400	CLASSIFICATION		GROUP		CLASS	'NLUC' closest equivalent NLUC code
1	2	3	4	5	6	Houses, Maisonettes, Flats, etc (other than Agricultural Dwelling Houses)	1	Bungalows	01 02	Bungalow Bungalows	RS02A-B -
1	2	3	4	5	6		2	Flats	01 02	Flat Flats	RS02A-A -
1	2	3	4	5	6		3	Houses	01 02	House Houses	RS02A -
1	2	3	4	5	6		4	Maisonettes	01 02	Maisonette Maisonettes	RS02A-D -
1	2	3	4	5	6		5	Parsonage Houses, etc	01 02 03 04	Parsonage Hse Dean's Hse Residentiary Canon's Hse Presbytery	RS02A-I RS02A-I RS02A-I RS02A-I
1	2	3	4	5	6		6	Reserved	01 to 99	)) reserved)	
1	2	3	4	5	6		7	Temporary Dwellings	01 02 03 04 05 06	Caravan and Pitch Chalet Dwelling Houseboat Room Rooms	RS01C-B RS02A-C RS02A RS01C-A RS01
1	2	3	4	5	6		8	Apartment Flatlet & Lodging Houses, Residential Homes & Rooms (See sec 115 & Sch 13 of G.R.A. 1967)	01 02 03 04 05 06 07 08	Apartment Hse Flatlet Hse Hostel Lodging Hse Residential Home House adapted for occupation in parts Aged Person's Home Old People's Home	RS02A-F RS02A-A RS01B-E RS02A-A RS01B-E RS01 CM04A-C CM04A-C
1	2	3	4	5	6		9	Stately Homes	01 02	Mansion Hse Castle	RS02A-1 RS02A-1

						'NLUC'
1	Shops assessed with Private Dwelling Accommodation	1	Shops & Shop Type Premises with Private Dwelling Accommodation	01	Shop	RT01
				02	Shops	-
				03	Bakery	RT01A-A
				04	Betting Office	LE01C-B
				05	Launderette	RT02B-C
				06	Surgery	CM01A
				07	Surgeries	-
				08	Consulting Room	CM01A
				09	Consulting Rooms	-
		2	Other Shop Type Premises with Private Dwelling Accommodation	01	Bank	OF02A-A
				02	Beauty Salon	RT01B-A
				03	Cafe	RT03B-B
				04	Dairy	RT01A-D
				05	Hairdressing Salon	RT01B-F
				06	Showroom	RT01C
				07	Showrooms	-
				08	Snack Bar	RT03B-B
				09	Off-Licence	RT01A-K
2	Shops (including Banks in Shopping Areas) Cafes & Restaurants	1	Shops & Supermarkets	01	Shop	RT01
				02	Shops	-
				03	Supermarket	RT01F-D
				04	Bakery	RT01A-A
				05	Off-Licence	RT01A-K
				06	Dairy	RT01A-D
				07	Hairdressing Salon	RT01B-F
				08	Launderette	RT02B-C
				09	Beauty Salon	RT01B-A
		2	Banks & Offices in shopping areas	01	Bank	OF02A-A
				02	Betting Office	LE01C-B
				03	Office	OF
				04	Offices	-
				05	Consulting Room	CM01A
				06	Consulting Rooms	-
		3	Cafes, Refreshment Rooms etc.	01	Cafe	RT03B-B
				02	Refreshment Room	RT03B-B
				03	Refreshment Rooms	-
				04	Auto Diner	RT03B-B
				05	Snack Bar	RT03B-B
				06	Tea Room	RT03B-B
				07	Tea Rooms	-
				08	Transport Cafe	RT03B-B

						'NLUC'
2		4	Departmental Stores & Showrooms	01	Department Store	RT01F-B
				02	Showroom	RT01C
				03	Showrooms	-
		5	Hypermarkets	01	Hypermarket	RT01F-C
		6	Kiosks & Photographic Booths	01	Kiosk	
				02	Kiosks	
				03	Photographic Booth	
				04	Photographic Booths	
		7	Other Shops etc	01	Bookstall	RT01B-N
				02	Handicraft Centre	RT01B-N
				03	Reserved	
				04	Studio	OF04A-A
				05	Studios	-
				06	Trading Centre	RT01F-A
				07	Garden Centre	RT01B-N
				08	Surgery	CM01A
				09	Surgeries	-
		8	Shop Ancillaries	01	Fitting Room	
				02	Fitting Rooms	
				03	Preparation Room	
				04	Preparation Rooms	
				05	Stock Room	
				06	Stock Rooms	
				07	Strong Room	
				08	Strong Rooms	
3	Offices (including Banks in Office Areas)	1	Offices	01	Office	OF
				02	Offices	-
		2	Banks in Office Area	01	Bank	OF02A-A
		3	Centres	01	Computer Centre	OF01A-E
				02	Driving Test Centre	OF01A-E
				03	Building Centre	OF01A-E
		4	Specific Offices	01	Betting Office	LE01C-B
				02	Booking Office	RT01B-L
				03	Employment Exchange	OF01A-E
				04	Estate Office	OF01A-E
				05	Inspectors Office	OF01A-E
				06	Ticket Office	RT01B-K
				07	Transport Office	RT01B-L

					'NLUC'
Factories, Mills & other premises of a similar character	1	Factories,etc	01	Factory	MA
			02	Factories	.
			03	Beet Sugar Factory	MA02A-K
			04	Coke Ovens	MA01A-A
	2	Mills	01	Mill	MA02A-H
			02	Flour Mill	MA02A-H
			03	Flour & Provender Mill	MA02A-H
			04	Provender Mill	MA02A-H
			05	Saw Mill	MA07A-B
			06	Paper Mill	MA07A-C
			07	Textile Mill	MA05A
	3	Works & Workshops	01	Works	
			02	Workshop	
			03	Workshops	
			04	Aircraft Works	MA04E-A
			05	Artificial Fibre Works	MA05A-F
			06	Motor Vehicle Works	MA04E-D
			07	Chemical Works	MA03A-D
			08	Printing Works	MA07B-D
			09	Joinery Works	MA07A-E
	4	Brick, Tile & Pipe Works, Kilns & Potteries	01	Brickworks	MA06A-B
			02	Brick & Pipe Works	MA06A-B
			03	Brick & Tile Works	MA06A-B
			04	Kiln	MA06A
			05	Kilns	-
			06	Kiln House	MA06A
			07	Tile Works	MA06A
			08	Pipe Works	MA06A
			09	Pottery	MA06A-E
	5	Asphalt Works Breeze Block Works, Concrete Batching Plants & Concrete Block Works	01	Asphalt Works	MA06A-A
			02	Breeze Block Works	MA06A-A
			03	Concrete Batching Plant	MA06A-A
			04	Concrete Block Works	MA06A-A
			05	Cement Works	MA06A-C
			06	Iron Works	MA01B-C
			07	Steel Works	
			08	Aluminium Works	MA01B-A
			09	Tinplate Works	MA01B-E
	6	Breweries, Maltings Bakeries & Dairies	01	Brewery	MA02A-E
			02	Malting	MA02A-E
			03	Maltings	-
			04	Bakery	MA02A-D
			05	Dairy	MA02A-I

						'NLUC'
1		7	Ship Building & Repair	01	Boat Repair Yard	MA04D-A
				02	Boat Yard	TR04A-B
				03	Dock Yard	TR02B-C
				04	Dry Dock	MA04D-A
				05	Dry Docks	-
				06	Repair Berth	MA04D-A
				07	Repair Berths	-
				08	Shipbuilding Yard	MA04D-A
				09	Ship Repairing Yard	MA04D-A
		8	Boiler Houses, Meter Houses & Rooms, Washing & Grading Plants & Curing Houses	01	Boiler House	MA04A-C ?
				02	Boiler Houses	-
				03	Meter House	
				04	Meter Houses	
				05	Meter Room	
				06	Meter Rooms	
				07	Washing Plant	AG07A-G
				08	Grading Plant	AG07A-G
				09	Curing House	AG07A-G
		9	Drying Rooms, Engine Sheds, Hoppers, etc	01	Drying Room	AG07A
				02	Drying Rooms	-
				03	Engine Shed	TR02C
				04	Engine Sheds	-
				05	Hopper	
				06	Hoppers	
				07	Test Track	TR01E-E
				08	Boiler Works	MA04A-C
				09	Locomotive Works	MA04E-B
		0	Other industrial Undertakings, etc	01	Oil Refinery	MA01A-C
				02	Forge	MA01B-C
				03	Foundry	MA01B-C
				04	Film Studio	LE01D-A
				05	Film Studios	-
				06	Laundry	RT02B-C
				07	Tannery	MA05B-C
				08	Slaughter House	AG03C-A
				09	Test House	
2	Mineral Producing Hereditaments (other than National Coal Board Hereditaments assessed under S35 2(a) General Rate Act 1967)	1	Brine Wells	01	Brine Well	MI01B-C
				02	Brine Wells	-
		2	Chalk Pits	01	Chalk Pit	MI01A-A
				02	Chalk Pits	-
		3	Clay Pits, Marl Pits	01	Clay Pit	MI01A-C
				02	Clay Pits	-
				03	Marl Pit	MI01A-H
				04	Marl Pits	-

TABLE 2

Proposed Secondary Descriptions of the Valuation List

Some examples of the draft coding index.

Secondary Descriptions from the Inland Revenue Valuation Office (1975)

- CAFE FLAT GARAGE & PREMISES 0180
- CAFE FLAT & PREMISES 0181
- CAFE FLATS & PREMISES 0182
- CAFE GARAGE & PREMISES 0183
- CAFE HOUSE GARAGE & PREMISES 0184
- CAFE HOUSE & PREMISES 0185
- CAFE MAISONETTE GARAGE & PREMISES 0186
- CAFE MAISONETTE & PREMISES 0187
- CAFE OFFICE & PREMISES 0188
- CAFE PETROL FILLING STATION HOUSE & PREMISES 0189
- CAFE & PREMISES 0190
- CAFE PUBLIC CONVENIENCES & PREMISES 0191
- CAFE WORKSHOP & PREMISES 0192
- CAFETERIA SHOPS & PREMISES 0193
- & CANTEEN 0194
- CANTEEN & PREMISES 0195
- CANTEEN & STORE 0196
- CANTEEN & STORES 0197
- CANTEEN STORES & PREMISES 0198
- CANTEEN STORES WORKSHOP & PREMISES 0199
- & CAR PARK 0200
- CAR PARK & CHANGING ROOM 0201
- CAR PARK & CHANGING ROOMS 0202
- CAR PARK HOUSE & PREMISES 0203
- CAR PARK & PREMISES 0204
- & CAR PORT 0205
- & CAR PORT (AG) 0206
- & CAR PORT (PR) 0207
- CAR PORT & GARAGE 0208
- CAR PORT & PREMISES 0209
- CAR PORT & STORE 0210
- CAR PORT & SWIMMING POOL 0211
- & CAR PORTS (2) 0212
- & CAR PORTS (3) 0213
- & CAR PORTS (4) 0214
- & CAR PORTS (5) 0215
- CAR PORTS & PREMISES 0216
- & CAR SPACE 0217
- & CAR SPACES 0218

- TELEPHONE EXCHANGE & PREMISES 0901
- & TELEVISION RELAY STATION 0902
- & TELEVISION RELAY SYSTEM 0903
- & TENNIS COURT 0904
- TENNIS COURT & PREMISES 0905
- & TENNIS COURTS 0906
- TENNIS COURTS BOWLING GREEN & PUTTING GREEN 0907
- TENNIS COURTS & PREMISES 0908
- THEATRE BALLROOM & PREMISES 0909
- TIMBER YARD & PREMISES 0910
- & TIP 0911

- (UNDER RE-CONSTRUCTION) 0912
- (UNFINISHED) 0913
- (USED AS NURSERY SCHOOL) 0914
- (USED AS STORE) 0915
- (USED FOR NON-MILITARY PURPOSES) 0916

- VEHICLE PARK & PREMISES 0917
- (VOID) 0918

- & WAITING ROOM 0919
- WAITING ROOM & PREMISES 0920
- WAITING ROOMS & PREMISES 0921
- & WALKS 0922
- WARDEN'S FLAT & PREMISES 0923
- WAREHOUSE FLAT & PREMISES 0924
- WAREHOUSE GARAGE & PREMISES 0925

REFERENCE MATERIAL

REFERENCE MATERIAL

The major part of this list is arranged under the local authorities who participated in this project (and in alphabetical order). Some more general references then follow.

We have not been able to find full bibliographic details of all the local authority sources; many of them are unpublished.

Specific local authority references

City of Birmingham District Council:

Development of a Computerised Information System within the Birmingham District Council Authority, Planning Department, R.W.M. Kedge et alia, June 1974.

General Enquiry System: System Description, P.J. Daniel, S.J. Harvey, July 1975.

Land Use Classification, Planning Department.

Cheshire County Council:

County Structure Plan: Revised Project Report, November 1974.

County Structure Plan: Report on Participation and Consultation, January 1975.

County Structure Plan: Progress Report Part I, February 1975.

County Structure Plan: Progress Report Part II, Policy Review and Appendix 2 Statistical Background, April 1975.

Development Potential: Opportunities and Constraints, Planning Department, Discussion Paper, 1974.

District "write-ups" 1-8, Planning Department Discussion Paper, 1974.

Housing and Industrial Land Information 'Systems' Manual, Planning Department, 1975.

Input Coding Manual for the Physical Environment File, Planning Department, 1975.

Planning Applications Computer System: User Manual - Input, Planning Department, 1975.

Town Centre Position Statements: Structure Plan Phase 4, Planning Department Discussion Paper, 1975.

Your Move - Towards Cheshire's Structure Plan, 1975.

1971 Census of Population: User Manual for Ward and Parish Library, Planning Department.

City of Coventry District Council:

City of Coventry Structure Plan 1973, April 1973.

Coventry City Policy Plan 1975: Survey Reports, Confidential, June 1975.

Coventry Land Use Classification: Hierarchical Classification of Lane Use Names and Codes, Department of Architecture and Planning, 2nd Edition, December 1973.

Coventry 66: The Making of a Development Plan, 1966.

Eagle Street Action Area Plan, April 1973.

Land Resource and Programme Division 1: Information Requirements, March 1971.

Survey Report: Land Resources, 1975.

System Manuals: Polygon Search Suite Analysis of Census Data, Computer Division City Treasurer's Department, 1974.

The Point Data System Report, March 1971.

East Lothian District Council:

County Planning Policy: Planning Department, County Planning Officer, May 1974.

Housing Sites Report 1974: County of East Lothian Review of Development Plan, Planning Department, 1974.

Population Report, Planning Department, September 1974.

City of Edinburgh District Council:

Applications for Planning Permission: Plans required, Planning Department, May 1975.

Graphic Data Information System, Planning Department, March 1972.

Information Systems Development, Edinburgh Corporation, April 1974.

The Graphic Data Handling System SJCIS/26, Scottish Development Department, Procedures and Methods Group, October 1971.

Gwent County Council:

Chepstow Inner Relief Road Stage Two: Choice of Route - We Need Your Views, Welsh Office Roads Division, March 1975.

Development Control Record Card: Guidance Notes for Completion of the Card, March 1974.

Gwent Management of Rural Roadside Verges, May 1975.

Gwent Planning Annual Report 1974, Planning Department, March 1975.

Gwent Plan Recreation and Tourism Discussion Paper No. 6, Planning Department, Draft 1975.

Gwent Plan Shopping Discussion Paper No. 8, Planning Department, Draft 1975.

Gwent Structure Plan Project Report, January 1975.

Monmouthshire Land Use Transportation Study: Main Report, Transportation Planning Associates and Monmouthshire County Planning Department, 1973.

Monmouthshire Land Use Transportation Study: Technical Report, Transportation Planning Associates and Monmouthshire County Planning Department, April 1974.

Monmouthshire Social Malaise Study: An Intertim Report on the Distribution of Social Problems, Joint Report of Planning Office and Department of Social Services, March 1974.

Hampshire County Council:

Blackwater Valley: Landscape. A joint report by Berkshire, Hampshire and Surrey County Councils, Draft 1975.

Geographic Data Processing - a Users Experience: Land Development Progress System, T. Gould, paper given at IBM Seminar on Geographic Data Processing 14-15 November, 1974.

Hampshire Summary of Statistics, A.D.G. Smart, County Planning Officer, September 1974.

Land Development Progress System: System Report, Planning Department, Draft July 1973.

South Hampshire Structure Plan: Summary of Draft Document for Participation and Consultation, South Hampshire Plan Advisory Committee, September 1972.

The Land Development Progress System: Use of the System, Planning Department, 1974.

Kensington & Chelsea Royal Borough Council:

Hotels and Tourism, Context Paper 4, 1975.

1971 Land Use Survey: CLUSTER 1 Survey Codes Full Print, Planning Service.

Lambeth Borough Council:

CLUSTER (Lambeth) Paper 1: General Description, Intelligence Unit of Department of Planning and Transportation, GLC in conjunction with CLPC.

CLUSTER: Centralon Land Use System and Employment Register: Papers 2 and 4, Instructions to Surveyors, June 1971 and later.

Computer Services in Lambeth, Computer division of the Directorate of Management Services, 1975.

Planning Information in Lambeth, Directorate of Development Services, August 1974.

City of Leeds District Council:

Clerical Instructions for UPRNing Leeds Metropolitan District - 6B, Database Operations Central Control, Merrion Centre, May 1974.

LAMIS (Local Authority Management Information System): A guide to the "Whys", "Whats" and "Wherefores" of the Land and Property Database currently being developed at Leeds.

LAMIS Project description, September 1974.

Leeds City Council: Planning Statistics, Department of Planning, February 1975.

Otley Local Plan: Draft Report of Survey, Department of Planning, May 1975.

60

City of Manchester District Council:

Availability of Land Use and Employment Data: Information Paper No. 1,
    Research Section, Information and Intelligence Group, Planning
    Department, February 1974.
City of Manchester: Census Information, Planning Department, 1975.
Manchester Land Use System: Land Use Search Routines, Planning
    Department.

Merseyside County Council:

A Review of Environmental Pollution in Merseyside, Report of the County
    Planning Officer, Public Protection Committee, March 1975.
Croxteth Park: A Preliminary Report of the Director of Museums and the
    County Planning Officer, 1975.
Development Control Arrangement, January 1974.
Instructions for Completing Planning Applications: General Information
    Form, Planning Department Information Unit, October 1974.
Merseyside - A Review as a Preliminary to the Preparation of a Joint
    Structure Plan. Merseyside Planning Officers' Group on Structure
    Planning, June 1972.
Merseyside County Council Development Plan Scheme, April 1975.
Tour of Ad. Hoc sites by the Merseyside County Planning Committee,
    Audrey M. Lees, County Planning Officer, June 1974.
Tour of Knowsley Metropolitan District by the County Planning Committee,
    Audrey M. Lees, County Planning Officer, August 1974.
Tour of St. Helen's Metropolitan District by the County Planning
    Committee, Audrey M. Lees, County Planning Officer, September 1974.
Tour of Sefton Metropolitan District by the County Planning Committee,
    Audrey M. Lees, County Planning Officer, October 1974.
Tour of Wirral Metropolitan District by the County Planning Committee,
    Audrey M. Lees, County Planning Officer, May 1974.

Mid Glamorgan County Council:

A County Management Information System (M.I.S.), 1973.
Caerphilly Local Plan Town Centre: Report of Survey and Appraisal
    Vol. 1 Main Findings, Glamorgan County Council Planning Department,
    July 1972.
Carboniferous Limestone. Long Term Reserves for Quarrying in Mid and
    South Glamorgan, Consultative Report, Mid Glamorgan County Council
    and South Glamorgan County Council Structure Plan Studies, March 1974.
Glamorgan County Council Strategy for Gower. County Planning
    Department, 1973.
Glamorgan County Council Structure Plan Studies: Strategy Generation,
    County Planning Department, 1973.
Management Information System. Report of the Sub-group to the Chief
    Officers' Management Information System Working Party, Glamorgan
    County Council, December 1971.
Mid Glamorgan County Council. Country Structure Plan Consultative
    Report: Planning Problems in Mid Glamorgan, Planning Office,
    November 1974.
Planning Applications Computer System: Systems Manual Vol. 1, 1974.
The Taff Valley: A basis for Action, County Planning Department
    Consultative Document, May 1973.

City of Newcastle-upon Tyne District Council:

Conserving Historic Newcastle: A Planning guide, Joint Conservation
Team of the City Council and Tyne and Wear Council under the
direction of Roy M. Angell, Planning Officer, 1975.
Current Projects: June 1975, Central Research Unit.
Papers by the Planning Department -
    Information Available from GISP   1972
    General Information System for Planning (GISP) 1973
    General Information System for Planning: Why? 1971
Planning Progress and Policy 1973: Newcastle-upon-Tyne, Kenneth A.
Galley, City Planning Officer, The Corporation Printing Section, 1973.
National Gazetteer Pilot Study: Land Use Classification, Tyne and
Wear County Council, January 1975.

Norfolk County Council:

Broadland Study and Plan, Report of Broads Consortium Committee
to the Broads Consortium, October 1971.
Decisions Analysis System Land Use Classification,
Planning Department, November 1974.
Information Services and Monitoring Sub-group: Report on
Land Availability Records, 1974.
Norwich Southern By-pass Environmental Survey, Planning Department 1974.
Planning Decisions Analysis Scheme: A report by the Planning
Department, October 1974.

A County Structure Plan 1975: A Consultative Draft,
East Sussex County Council, February 1975.

Mapping and handling of land use and related information:

A Cartographic Editing System Applied to Soil Mapping in the Netherlands,
Colin White, Commission III Technical Working Session of the
International Cartographic Association, Netherlands, April 1975.
Automatic Cartography and Planning, E.C.U., Architectural Press 1971.
Automatic Cartography and Urban Data Banks in the U.K., D.W. Rhind
and T.C.G. Trewman, 7th International Cartographic Association
Conference, Madrid, 1974.
Census Information Retrieval and Analysis System: User Guide,
Prepared by M.J. Gibson, Revised by J.R. Pinnington, Hoskyns
Systems Ltd., July 1974.
Geographical Data Handling, R.F. Tomlinson (ed) 2 vols, IGU Commission
on Geographic Data Sensing and Processing for the UNESCO/IGU
Second Symposium on Geographical Information Systems, Ottawa, 1972.
(Bibliographic).
GIMMS: An example of an Operational System for Computer Cartography,
T.C. Waugh and D.R.F. Taylor,   published in the December 1976
issue of The Canadian Cartographer.
GIMMS: Users Manual, Susan Richer, Department of Geography,
Carleton University, Ottawa, August 1976.

Graphical Representation of Data from Geographical Information Systems,
Proc. of the Conference of RTPI, LAMSAC and NCC, London,
April 1973.

I. B. M. Geographic Information Project: Tees-side, E. C. U.,
November 1974.

Interactive Cartography at the E. C. U., S. B. M. Bell and D. P. Bickmore,
Commonwealth Survey Officers' Conference, Paper No. J6, 1975.

Improving the quality of automated thematic maps, A. Buchanan and
G. A. Hackman, 7th International Cartographic Association Conference,
Madrid, 1974.

Land Parcel Identifiers for Information Systems, D. David Moyer and
Kenneth Paul Fisher, American Bar Federation, Chicago, 1973
(Bibliographic).

Reference Manual for Synagraphic Computer Mapping: SYMAP,
Harvard Laboratory for Computer Graphics, Version V, 1968.

Thematic Mapping by Computer, G. M. Gaits, Cartographic Journal,
June 1969.

Other relevant research studies:

General Information System for Planning, Joint Local Authority,
Scottish Development Department and DOE study team, HMSO, 1972.

General Review of Local Authority Management Information Systems
Research Report 1, McKinsey and Co. Inc. for the Secretary of State
for the Environment, DOE 1975.

Manual on Point Referencing of Properties and Parcels of Land,
Department of Environment, HMSO 1973.

Memoranda of the Co-ordinating Committee on Locational Referencing:
National Gazetteer Pilot Study, DOE 1974/75.

National Land Use Classification, Joint Local Authority LAMSAC,
SDD and DOE Study Team, DOE 1975.

Point-in-Polygon Project Stage 1: Research Report 2, James, Heard
and Suttie for Secretary of State for the Environment, DOE 1975.

The Valuation List:

Local Government Finance: Report of the Committee of Enquiry,
Chairman Frank Layfield QC, Cmnd 6453 HMSO May 1976.

Primary Descriptions of the Valuation List: the Draft Hierarchical
List of Codes, Inland Revenue Valuation Officer, 1975.

Secondary Descriptions of the Valuation List - the Draft Coding Index,
Inland Revenue Valuation Office, 1975.

General:

Development Plans. A Manual on Form and Content, Ministry of
Housing and Local Government, and Welsh Office, HMSO 1970.

Information Needs of Planners: a Survey, Erlet Cater, Urban Systems
Research Unit, University of Reading, USRU-WP-4, July 1970.

Land Use Statistics in the United Kingdom, J. T. Coppock,
University of Edinburgh, 1975.

Local Government in England and Wales: A Guide to the New System, DOE and Welsh Office, HMSO 1974.

Statistics of Town and County Planning, L. F. Gebbett, Interim Report, 1975.

Town and County Planning Act 1971, HMSO 1974.